The Frustrated Raider

THE STORY OF THE GERMAN CRUISER

Cormoran

IN WORLD WAR I

By Charles Burdick

Southern Illinois University Press

Carbondale and Edwardsville

Feffer & Simons, Inc. : London and Amsterdam

Library of Congress Cataloging in Publication Data

Burdick, Charles Burton, 1927–
    The frustrated raider.

    Bibliography: p.
    Includes index.
    1. Cormoran (Ship)   2. European War, 1914–1918—Naval operations,
German.   3. European War, 1914–1918—Pacific Ocean.   I. Title

D582.C67B87   940.4′59′43   78-12857.
ISBN 0-8093-0899-1

To Donna, Jackie, Janice, Karol, and Teri
for listening

Contents

Illustrations

Acknowledgments

This is an adventure story of a ship and her crew in the maelstrom of war. While the *Cormoran* did not leave any grandiose events for Mars's chronicles, she did provide insight into the exhilaration, the foibles, and the human dimension of war. The *Cormoran*'s skillful, daring, and successful efforts to survive both against superior force and cantankerous administrative controls provide a historical vignette for human study.

To those kind persons who have given time, consideration, and advice I am most grateful. One must hope that the following pages help repay that debt in some small way.

Among the many archivists who have contributed to the story, I am particularly indebted to Fregattenkapitan a.D. Heinz von Bassi (Muerwik); Fregattenkapitan a.D. August Wilhelm Heye (Marine-Offizier-Vereinigung); Dr. Sandhofer (Bundesarchiv); John Taylor and Gibson Smith (National Archives); Joyce Eakin (U.S. Army Military History Institute); Agnes Peterson (the doyenne of helpers at the Hoover Institution provided, as she always does, the selfless devotion which makes scholarship a happy experience).

Other individuals who have helped with the project include Bea Gormley who read it in detail; Fritz Bayer, Andrew Lassen, Herbert Ward, and Carmelita Ortiz who shared experiences; Clayton Trost, Norbert Sopolsky, and King Wah Moberg who searched for books.

Irmgard von Waaden, Marlene Bosanko, Cia Oropeza, Ilse and Donald Detwiler, Robert Johnson, and Gerald Wheeler provided guidance and comfort at various times. Ms Mimi T. Negendank did the Index as a labor of love. The Alexander von Humboldt Stiftung and its leaders, Heinrich Pfeiffer and Thomas Berberich, provided the intellectual atmosphere and economic support allowing this publication. Certainly they must accept credit for any value in this book; the errors belong to the author.

Charles Burdick

San José State University
San Jose, California
July 14, 1978

The Frustrated Raider

Chapter 1 German Colonial and Naval Policies

In 1884 the chancellor of the German Empire, Otto von Bismarck, finally approved a national pursuit of colonies. After thirteen years of resistance to the pressures of aggressive businessmen, the blandishments of eager chauvinists, and the proclamations of various pressure groups, Bismarck turned to overseas territorial acquisition. With a young, recently unified country behind him the Iron Chancellor's decision brought rapid implementation. Perhaps the most cogent statement for this expansion came through the German Colonial Society, formed in 1882, with its program for colonization: 1) a source for acquiring raw materials and a place for marketing finished products; 2) an outlet for investing German capital; 3) a visible symbol of German power and international prestige; 4) a place to export surplus population. This concept provided for enthusiastic popular support and for the emotional environment required for rapid aggrandizement.

While Germany started the European game of "African grab" almost immediately, German adventurers turned to Asia as well. In December 1884 Bismarck informed other European powers that the German Empire would protect the northern coast of New Guinea (Kaiser Wilhelm's Land). Thereafter he extended protectorate status to many islands scattered across the Pacific. These odds and ends of leftover coral reefs, unwanted islands, and little-explored places created an image of empire if not a reality. In less than two years the German kaiser, Wilhelm II, could point to various specks on the map as his property although most of them seemed scarcely large enough to carry the national flag. While this hastily assembled empire provided a lure for economic and political aspiration, it also provided a very real military liability.

The scattered protectorates required both the occasional image and sometimes the prompt reality of German military force. Because of the extensive distances involved with these activities only the navy could provide these services. For an infant service struggling to develop a sense of professionalism, to increase its ships in both quantity and quality, and to locate a path out of its strategic isolation these additional challenges created harsh problems. Few of the colonies had any relationship to naval strategic realities or logistical requirements; they represented the needs of the spirit rather than those of the fist. The German outposts in the Pacific lacked harbors suitable as natural naval anchorages. To make them useful would require a vast financial commitment for dredging, construction, and maintenance. In addition the sheer responsibility for patroling the acquisitions, showing the flag in foreign harbors, and coordinating everything created dilemmas far beyond the authority of the new navy. Clearly the last decade of the nineteenth century demanded solutions to many questions.

The fleet expansion program competed for national resources with the army and its victorious heritage. For some years the navy lost this contest for funds but the young, impetuous, arrogant Kaiser Wilhelm II's arrival in 1888 changed the rules. Much impressed by the American writer Alfred T. Mahan the kaiser wanted a more effective naval force. He and his naval advisers confronted two overriding difficulties in their deliberations. The first was the obvious concern for the fleet's potential employment in time of war; the second was coping with the technological innovations impacting on naval shipping, especially those relative to the transition from sail to steam.

Within Germany the former issue created a sharp division among the participating leaders. Given the obvious truth that a German fleet required many years before it could compete with the Royal Navy in raw numbers, the planners required a sophisticated strategy utilizing finesse. From this fact came two schools of thought drawn from the common study of the Napoleonic Wars. The one envisaged a powerful, centralized battle fleet concentrated in the homeland for action against continental opponents. The Napoleonic efforts to overcome France's naval deficiencies vis-à-vis England's authority through individual corsairs and privateers brought no lasting rewards. This globular effort had failed its purpose because Albion understood the main battle area and never let up the pressure at that point.

This substantive view, despite powerful adherents like Adm. Alfred Tirpitz, confronted a distinctly contrary opinion. The supporters of this concept drew attention to the European land mass and the ease with which a modest power (which England was not) could blockade Germany. These people held that even the most powerful fleet centered in German ports could not escape ignominious defeat. They posited the thought that Germany's geographic position was much different from that of France and necessitated cruisers for far-flung operations against enemy supply lines, shipping, and prestige. In addition such operations would spread out a powerful enemy's marine units for easier destruction, embarrass his government, and allow meaningful successes against food supplies, munitions, and raw materials. With a hard-hitting, adventuresome assault any opponent would fall victim to the individual barbs.

These two views provided questions demanding a simple, effective answer for German naval development and strategy. In the years down to 1914 no one allowed this requirement to reach directional fruition. As the alternatives oscillated back and forth, the indecisive kaiser shifted his ground between them. As the final judge in this struggle for position and authority he shifted his ground in accordance with his latest discussion. The failure of decision doomed Germany to eventual disaster.

For the cruiser-warfare idea this indecision was more difficult than for the home fleet concept. Few officers based in Berlin could envisage the potential loss of new, modern vessels in a distant clime. At the same time assigning antiquated or outmoded units risked ineffectiveness, defeat, and damaging loss without result. This qualitative problem of where to assign the best fighting ships —assuming that a war would not allow a careful order—added a significant dimension to the argument.

Behind this unresolved dilemma was the technological revolution. Bismarck had once remarked, with sarcastic intent, "We have a fleet that is unable to sail, so we cannot be injured in distant parts of the world." Even as he expressed these views of his antiquated naval force, the introduction of the coal-burning steam engine forced change. It provided opportunities for overcoming nature, for increased firing power, and improved ship design. While permitting these all-encompassing changes, the "black gold" was not an efficient fuel. Coal consumption increased in a geometric rather than an arithmetic ratio as speed increased. Foul weather, enemy action, or any undue activity shortened a vessel's range to the point where replenishment was a weekly event. The taking on of coal was not a happy occurrence for any ship's complement. With any vessel the undertaking was cumbersome, dangerous, dirty, and unpleasant. It demanded sufficient stability that transfering coal on the high seas was, essentially, an impossible task. In even a remote, hidden cove the time-consuming procedure made a war vessel impotent and vulnerable to surprise. Clearly a coal-burning ship demanded a consistent, available source of high-grade coal as well as convenient depots and loading facilities.

Given such considerations any cruiser war forced Germany to develop overseas bases for commerce raiders. The new possessions lacked the potential for these bases and forced the cruiser-war supporters to seek new bases and techniques in the face of declining sites. For many years German vessels cruised the Pacific secretly mapping strange islets and atolls, investigating useful locations for refitting vessels, and searching out hiding places for wartime use. The ships' officers sketched landforms, took soundings, and triangulated precise locations. Nonetheless, while the expanding German navy could show the Imperial Eagle flag in many Asian ports, the crew could not usefully employ their native language ashore. Germany owned no harbor worthy of such designation and, ultimately, had to find one, or more, in East Asia, some 10,000 nautical miles from the homeland.

After lengthy effort the Germans seized a ready-made opportunity to take the Kiaochow Bay area on China's Shantung peninsula. In 1897, reacting to the murder of two missionaries, three small German naval units, *Kaiser*, *Prinzess Wilhelm*, and *Cormoran* landed a small expeditionary force. Acting with undue haste German diplomats consummated the contractual agreements providing control of a 500-square kilometer area. The new protectorate, together with its natural harbor, Tsingtao came under naval control. Working to show efficiency and authority the navy rapidly turned the small village into a modern installation. Travel brochures carried the enviable descriptive titles of "the Asian Brighton," "Pearl of the East," and "the Eastern Riviera" as German efficiency created a major naval base and tourist attraction. While a distinctive beginning, Tsingtao did not resolve the complications posed by distance and new scientific innovations.

The discoveries in communication occasioned prompt difficulties for the raider idea. Oceanic cables allowed rapid communication over long distances and necessitated changes in diplomatic, commercial, and military activity. Since England controlled most of the cable networks, that government would restrict message security in wartime. For isolated German cruisers in Asia these octopus tentacles spelled difficult—if not fatal—discovery.

The wireless provided another intimidating influence for individual cruisers. While it was limited in range and expanded navigational error, the wireless provided an audible, traceable device as well as a means of communication. The ubiquitous machine allowed a commerce raider to communicate with its required colliers but revealed the colliers' locations to destructive hunters. Additionally any attacked merchantman could attract a noisome crowd within a short time and force an attacker, no matter how successful, to steam away at high speed; with excessive coal consumption.

The advance of technology, the lack of defensible, useful bases (Tsingtao notwithstanding), the estrangement of long-term philosophical directions, and the continued intimidating press of England's presence confronted Germany with an unpleasant reality. With its power centered on the continent and on a flighty kaiser, Germany remained a powerful globular force without clear purpose, especially in Asia. The resultant flux within a known system and the plethora of shortsighted goals portended future trouble for everyone.

Within this uncertainty the members of the Asian power structure were also shifting about seeking better understanding. By 1914 Japan had joined the power structure by defeating the Russians, by diplomatic accord with England, and by territorial influence on the Asian mainland. They owned geographic location, powerful momentum, and political sophistication. The French and English had major economic interests, political influence in China, the traditional strength born of empire, and what they lacked in military authority they kept through presence and experience. The Russians kept up their involvement but, despite a major interest, they lacked the requisite means. A more recent member of the Asian power community was the United States. While essentially moralizing traders, the Americans with their exaggerated pride, growing diplomatic experience, and increasing economic authority altered essential power relationships. The Asian world of 1914 was a vast arena for competition, mistrust, and aggrandizement all taking place with unexpected haste.

For the participants the opportunity of growth overwhelmed understanding. The Germans confidently envisaged their future as one without limit. If they could keep up the needed payments in interest, treasure, and manpower, they could anticipate superlative returns. Still, they lacked the requisite physical authority, the broad military awareness, and the additional new vessels for modern warfare. In sum, they possessed a greedy appetite but their teeth were of poor quality.

Chapter 2 Beginning

On a steely gray December day in 1914 a small, weatherbeaten vessel stood in Apra Harbor in the Pacific island of Guam. As she moved slowly through the gentle waves of a peaceful ocean, the visitor showed unmistakable signs of fatigue and long travel. She rested high in the water, her waterline a clearly discernible mark riding well over the swells, mute testimony of her empty holds. The dark, under-laden smoke spiraling into the sky reflected a poor-quality fuel in the boiler fires. The hull, pockmarked with rust and the eroding scars of long-embedded salt spray, provided additional evidence of weeks of hard travel and inattention to the rules of professional maritime maintenance.

Along with this dubious image, however, were other symbols which explained the ship's disrepair. At the masthead a shredded naval ensign reflected both an allegiance and a pride. Also the polished gun barrels jutting out from various unexpected locations stated a determined purpose. As the newcomer moved closer to the shore, the name *Cormoran* stood out in bold relief, a contrastingly clean shield among the manifest signs of decay and age. While she appeared to be an apt candidate for the break-up yard, she was clearly armed and a warship of the Imperial German Navy.

The minuscule American colony resident on the island found itself confronted, after months of general solitude and insular boredom, with a genuine German raider. At first glance there was little about the newcomer to occasion the slightest concern. Despite the incessant press propaganda concerning the fabled predators of the sea, the tiny vessel wallowing in the harbor's quiet waters could scarcely bring tremors of fear to even the most timid observer. Nevertheless it was a cautious group of concerned

Americans who boarded the ship and found that the shabby appearance was not a sham; the Germans were not really in a position to threaten the island's security. Actually there were few pugnacious thoughts on board. To the raider's crew Guam was a delightful haven, safely removed from the rigors and threats of war. Behind them stretched hundreds of miles of frustration, uncertainty, near disaster, and fearful adventure. The American outpost was the welcome terminus of their Odyssean journey, begun many months earlier when the First World War had splintered the world's peaceful order.

The assassination of Archduke Francis Ferdinand in June 1914 had unexpectedly pushed Europe to the brink of war. Like all concerned national governments, German leaders had to consider the threat in all of its global implications. For the kaiser's government, aside from the immediate land struggle with its continental neighbors, war presented an instant threat to its far-flung colonial empire. In terms of both distance and difficulty of control, the remote Pacific area posed the most serious challenges. A vast ocean, dotted by odd-shaped bits and pieces of land, the Pacific remained a charted but mysterious zone. A glance at a map provided a false impression of order and propriety, of accessibility and control, of communication and protection. In reality the area was a wide, foreboding body of water which demanded a measure of courage and foolhardiness from every visitor. For war it provided a series of challenges to any defender because of its many geographic complexities, unusual distances, and unknown hydrographic details.

The German protectorates consisted of a strange assortment of properties, few of them possessing major significance, and each one only a second-rate decoration for the coat of nationalism. In the south the Germans controlled the northeast corner of New Guinea (Kaiser Wilhelm's Land) with the neighboring Bismarck Archipelago and a portion of the Solomon Islands. The major settlement was Friedrich Wilhelm's Harbor although even it did not possess a sizable group of Europeans. To the north they owned the Micronesian groups, including the Palaus, the Marianas, and the Caroline and Marshall islands. The political authority centered at Rabaul, a pleasant site adjacent to Blanche Bay on the coast of New Britain (Neu Pommern). In the extreme south the Germans had two large Samoan Islands, Savaii and Upolu, with Apia as the basic settlement. The properties were scattered over the seascape, and even an uneducated eye could see that the Germans owned the smallest and least important specks on the map. Around them were vast expanses of water and real estate either owned or controlled by powerful potential enemies.

In all cases Germany's land holdings supported only a limited white population in trading stations and plantations which dotted the coastlines with little regard for the interior areas. In view of this somewhat limited exploitation, the central authorities in Berlin developed a colonization plan to edge the coastline with tiny settlements linked together by good roads. On occasion certain more adventurous souls pushed inland to build individual empires in the jungle, but the vast majority of the settlers remained along the water's edge, content to leave the hinterland to its own unknown devices. So long as the native tribes kept a measure of order, paid a small tax, and avoided too much contact with the white settlers, they were left to themselves. Any exploration stemmed from scientific purposes. Many learned tomes on botany, zoology, and ethnology enriched the scholarly community, even if they did little to attract industrious colonists or curious tourists.

Communication between the islands and the outside world depended upon two sources. The major center for the submarine cable was the island of Yap. It had connections to Guam (and the United States), to Shanghai, and to Menado in the Celebes. Yap had served as the main telegraph station as well as the major center for wireless transmission throughout the German islands. Realizing the weakness of such singular centralization, the colonial authorities in Berlin had planned a connecting wireless link throughout the protectorates, but this system had not been completed by 1914. There were stations of varying power in Apia, Nauru, Yap, and Tsingtao in the north. The station at Nauru was the best one in terms of power and modern equipment. A secondary system at Rabaul was under construction, but lacked the necessary parts for distance transmission. There was a minor position at Angaur, a phosphate island in the Palau group, and a weak, privately owned unit at Truk and Jaluit in the Marshalls. By 1914 the island communities had some communication with each other and the homeland, but the system was weak in its power sources, its lack of coordination, and was obviously ill prepared for war.

The other means of communication were the passenger and freight traffic and the postal service. These needs were served by the ships of Austral-Japan Line and the Singapore-New Guinea subsidiary of the North-German Lloyd as well as various steam and sailing ships belonging to private business corporations. Three vessels of the Austral-Japan Line, the *Coblenz*, *Prinz Sigismund*, and *Prinz Waldemar*, sailed once a month for a round trip between Australia and Japan. En route they stopped in Sydney, Brisbane, and, in the protectorates, Rabaul, Friedrich Wilhelm's Harbor, Nauru, Yap, and Angaur. Thereafter they moved on to Manila, Hong Kong, and, ultimately, Kobe, Japan. A few vessels carrying phosphates from Nauru and Angaur also made occasional calls at sundry ports, but no foreign lines moved regularly through the protectorates. Obviously there were few exchanges between these semiwild islands and the outside world. The settlers were totally dependent upon Australia, Hong Kong, and Japan for all supplies, equipment, and food. At no place was there a viable independent economy.

Even more complex than the supply and communication issues was the protection question. Defense of the protectorates was a frightening problem, particularly in view of the possible opponents, distance from the homeland, and the poor quality of available military equipment and supplies. Australia and Japan were both ideally located to move against the Germans in a huge viselike pincers movement. Acting in union, they could use their forces like the jaws of an alligator to crush the totally exposed and vulnerable Germans. Any war would obviously place the protectorates on their own resources—enemy occupation of all inhabited areas was only a question of time rather than of strength. The Germans' local defense units consisted of a few, widely scattered constabulary groups, some local militiamen, and an expeditionary force of approximately 120 Negroes stationed near Rabaul for suppressing possible native uprisings. Obviously there was no formal army presence. Any attempt at establishing a defense system depended entirely upon whatever authority the German navy could muster in the area.

Obviously the Germans lacked any considerable maritime authority. Their navy depended upon two sources for maintaining the imperial ensign against foreign threats. Without question the most significant force was the Asiatic squadron based upon the impressively modern installation at Tsingtao. This port had been permanently occupied by the Germans in the late nineteenth century and continuously improved thereafter. By 1914 they had over $12,000,000 invested in its facilities and the resultant harbor was one worthy of a first-class naval power. These impressive docks and warehouses provided visual testimony to human effort and military planning, but they could not conceal two fundamental problems of protecting the German colonies.

The first was the simple question of geography. Tsingtao was ideally located for protecting German interests in China. Fleet units could move quickly along the Chinese coast or up the various rivers to a troubled area. Significantly, however, the squadron quartered there had the responsibility of defending the island empire as well. For that role, Tsingtao did not hold a functional position. From Tsingtao to Pagan, the most northern of the Marianas, was some 2,000 miles. Given the great distance between the protectorates and the South Pacific colonies, and the fact that ships of the time burned coal, warships based on Tsingtao faced extraordinary challenges in trying to defend the far-flung colonies. The movement of supplies, repair facilities, and simple navigational concerns imposed frightening logistical burdens upon German resources. Also vulnerable was the harbor's location in the Yellow Sea; should a significant naval power decide to cordon off that locality, it would have few problems in containing all shipping caught in the badly shaped area. The Japanese, in particular, had a strategic stranglehold on the mouth of the sack. With a minimum of confusion and strength, they could mount a total blockade beyond serious challenge.

Besides the location issue loomed the question of power itself. Kaiser Wilhelm II, the eager protagonist of German colonization, encouraged the speedy occupation of all available land. Defense costs were another matter. While the emperor accepted ever-increasing territorial responsibilities throughout the world, he and his legislative body were parsimonious in creating a naval establishment adequate to defend them. Since the Far East was most distantly removed from Berlin, the Asiatic squadron suffered more than other operational areas from outright neglect. In

1914 it possessed two heavy and three light cruisers. The *Scharn-horst* and *Gneisenau* served as the heavy elements. They were sister ships who, like human twins, varied in operational excellence. Each weighed 11,600 tons, and carried eight 8.2-inch guns and six 5.9-inch guns. They had been launched in 1906 and naval experts considered them among the most modern vessels of the day. The three light cruisers, *Leipzig*, *Nürnberg*, and *Emden*, varied in age, size, and power. The former, built in 1905, was the oldest, while the *Emden*, constructed in 1908, was the youngest. All carried ten 4.1-inch guns and made speeds in excess of twenty-three knots. Collectively, as a combat squadron, they possessed excellent speed, adequate armament, and sufficient power to make an impressive display as participants in a peacetime review.

Their ultimate authority, however, rested upon two factors of utmost import to any military mission. First, they were totally dependent upon vast quantities of coal for mobility. Their sole source for such fuel was Germany. Since they could not obtain any deposits in the Pacific, the vessels relied upon colliers, imports to Tsingtao, or sources in foreign ports. If they had sufficient early warning of war, the fleet might make adequate provisions; a surprise conflict would immediately threaten their essential coal supplies.

Second, and as important, was the issue of the protagonists; in the Pacific the arrangement of powers was such that Germany had to take into consideration a British contingent including Australia and New Zealand, the French, and the Japanese. Against the latter two, individually, there was some chance of success. Any combination of the three, or the British alone, was another matter—they would be too strong in any armed conflict. For the German fleet, therefore, the basic issues were preparation, limiting the number of enemies, and protecting a safe coal supply. In the first months of 1914, however, no one seriously considered the remote possibility of war.

A second and far more limited defense force was the local control authority. In peacetime the Imperial German Navy maintained two small cruisers and the supply and survey vessel *Planet* (650 tons with a speed of ten knots) in the South Pacific. Their main function was to keep the uneducated natives aware of omnipresent German authority and, if necessary, to intervene against outright rebellion or riot. As a result the two cruisers were constantly on the move and tried to keep a schedule permitting a semiannual visit to every German-held area. Since many of the lesser harbors, particularly those in the Coral Sea, contained numerous uncharted reefs, the navy used obsolete small cruisers which had passed the twenty-year service limitation imposed by German naval law, or whose design had been made obsolescent by technological progress. As a result the authorities demoted them to the less glamorous, if more proper, designation of gunboat.

In 1913 the two resident vessels were the *Condor* and the *Cormoran*, a well-matched pair for the job assigned to them. Built in 1892, they were sister ships of 1,630 tons with speeds in excess of fifteen knots, and carrying eight 4.1-inch guns. The crews curried their glistening white-painted vessels with obvious industry and pride. They maintained, as well, sails for use in sparing valuable coal and as stabilizers in rough weather. For their Eastern housekeeping role both ships served with distinction. In any naval action against modern foes, however, they manifestly could not compete to any significant extent.

During December 1913 the *Condor*, after eleven years of uninterrupted Pacific service, received orders to return home for proper retirement. She would be replaced in the course of the summer by a sister ship, the *Geier*, built in 1894 to the same plans. After the *Condor*'s departure, the *Cormoran* was, apart from the *Planet*, the sole warship on permanent station in the South Pacific.

She bore the challenge with pride. In fact the *Cormoran* had been deeply involved with the building of the German Pacific empire. In October 1897 some Chinese workers had thrown stones at some sailors off the *Cormoran*. The action had created a prompt retaliatory response by the ship's crew. When some bandits murdered two missionaries shortly afterwards, the kaiser ordered the occupation of Tsingtao. In the subsequent armed invasion, the *Cormoran*'s participation helped sway the engagement. Although later posted to East Africa for a lengthy service tour, her presence in the Far East served as a constant visual reminder of the German presence in Asia, its origins, and its tenure. She was therefore very busy attempting to show the German flag throughout the protectorates. As a result the crew had numerous extra duties to accompany their normal activities. In 1913 the *Cormoran* fulfilled her duty with a lengthy, official trip. She called at the normal ports, few of which offered any real pleasures, either to the intellect or to the senses. To give the crew some taste of civilization, the Berlin authorities arranged a five-day visit to the American outpost at Guam. The *Cormoran* docked on December 13 and the crew did enjoy their holiday.

Afterward, in February 1914, the ship's crew members made a week-long, extra-duty expedition through the southern portion of Bougainville Island in the Solomons, with the result that most of them contracted malaria. Thereafter, the ship had to lay over at Ponape in the Carolines, where the pleasant climate provided a leisurely rest cure for everyone. In this way the sick could recover a measure of health while the others enjoyed a rather lazy existence. Following this extensive rest period, the *Cormoran* moved on to Tsingtao for its normal annual refit and general overhaul. This stay was scheduled to last three months because the ship, after a five-year absence from Germany, required major repair. The crew, many still weak from the fever, looked forward to a pleasant period of shore duty. They would see many old friends in the Asiatic squadron and have sufficient freedom to enjoy them. However, they did not reckon with the aims of superior authority nor with the whims of international diplomacy.

For 1914 the German Asiatic fleet, under Adm. Maximilian Graf von Spee, had the *Scharnhorst, Gneisenau, Leipzig, Nürnberg*, and *Emden* as effective warships. It also controlled the gunboats *Vaterland, Tsingtao, Otter, Iltis, Luchs*, and *Tiger*. The first three were at posts on the Yangtze River; the others scattered around not far from Canton. In addition to the *Cormoran* there were the elderly torpedo boat *S-90* and a lightly armed steamer, the *Titania*, used for miscellaneous purposes. The limited size of this force precluded its permanent location in any one place. With a widely scattered ocean empire, von Spee had to keep his ships constantly in motion, checking on this harbor, appearing in that port, and generally keeping up a façade of authority and strength throughout the vast Pacific. Likewise he had additional responsibilities throughout the disparate harbors available to German use.

Not every ship could enter the coral-reef-encrusted, virtually unknown bays and inlets available as harbors. The larger, more modern naval units often had to anchor outside in technological frustration while an antiquated associate moved easily over the treacherous reefs into a pleasant anchorage. Spee had to plan with great care to keep his squadron on post while fulfilling these other obligations. His problem, then, was to be strong enough to stand against the challenge of any one or a combination of great powers, to spread out sufficiently to provide a protective umbrella for the protectorates, and to be flexible enough to combine quickly for immediate action along the mainland coast. Obviously his assignment was not an easy one. He could not afford to keep the *Cormoran*'s many friends in Tsingtao for prolonged social exchanges.

In 1914 von Spee decided that he would take his two heavy cruisers (*Scharnhorst* and *Gneisenau*) through the protectorates for a leisurely cruise. The trip was to replace an aborted planned exercise from the previous year when troubles in China had forced him to keep the big units available in Tsingtao. While he was gone this time the *Emden* would remain as a guard ship against possible Chinese difficulties. The *Leipzig* would move across the Pacific to replace the *Nürnberg* off the Mexican coast to show the German flag to the restless peoples of that region. *Nürnberg*, badly in need of overhaul, should return to Tsingtao for refit and general repair. The concept was a simple one, organized to satisfy normal naval considerations. Spee had no overriding reason to consider the possibility of war. If he had had reason even to remotely contemplate the possibility, he would have taken pause in view of his possible foes.

The Germans shared the Asiatic climes with four other major naval establishments. Of the four the Russians were the weakest and could scarcely count as a formidable opponent. They had suffered a morale-shattering, materially catastrophic defeat at the hands of the Japanese in 1904–5 and had not yet recovered either their physical or psychological strength. While their two cruisers, *Askold* and *Zhemchug*, and their assorted destroyers and submarines represented a useful force, they could pose no serious threat to anyone. The French had the armored cruiser *Montcalm* (completed in 1902 with two 7.6-inch and 6.4-inch guns, a displacement of 9,517 tons and a speed of twenty-one knots), and the armored cruiser *Dupleix* (finished in 1903 with eight 6.4-inch guns, a weight of 7,432 tons and a speed of just over twenty knots), along with some lesser units. Like the Russians the French could undertake significant action only in combination with other nations; alone they were not an impressive force.

The great Pacific powers were two—Great Britain and Japan. The former had one old battleship, the *Triumph* (built in 1904 with four 10-inch guns and fourteen 7.5-inch guns, a weight just short of 12,000 tons, and a speed of twenty knots), and two heavy cruisers, two light cruisers, eight destroyers, and a wide range of lesser units. With this force was aligned that of Australia, which was singularly impressive. At its head was the most impressive naval vessel in the Pacific, a massive battle cruiser, justifiably named after the country. She had been finished in 1911 with eight 12-inch guns in the main armament, a tonnage of 18,800 tons, and a speed of twenty-five knots. Alone, she could match her strength against any naval force in the Orient. In addition to this steel monster, the Australians had four light cruisers and three modern destroyers.

Finally came the Japanese, who owned six modern battleships and five older ones, six battle cruisers, eleven heavy cruisers, twelve light cruisers, and an armada of coastal vessels. With this respectable naval force and the victorious spirit born of the recent decision over Russia, the Japanese presented a formidable organization. This impressive assemblage alone was more than enough to isolate, engage, or destroy the German Asiatic fleet under von Spee.

The German naval authorities in Berlin fully realized that they could never meet a collective Pacific force with any hope of survival. For many years they had, therefore, planned essentially defensive measures in the event of war. The German admiralty hoped to develop a strategy founded upon cruiser warfare, where the essential mission was the greatest interruption to the enemy's establishment at the least risk to the raiding forces. This approach involved destroying the enemy's commerce and communications, protecting German supply lines, diverting the enemy's strength, and avoiding direct confrontation at all costs. Also, the available German naval strength should endeavor to protect its bases at Tsingtao and throughout the protectorates while assuring a sufficient fuel supply for every eventuality.

Chapter 3 Birth

The news from Europe concerning the death of the Austrian Archduke Francis Ferdinand reached Tsingtao on June 29, 1914. While the wanton murder created a general feeling of horror throughout the port, only a pessimistic handful of the residents seriously considered it a threat to international peace. Virtually all the city's cosmopolitan population agreed with the unanimous verdict of the local foreign government representatives—the mere idea of international conflict was nonsensical. Austria might, understandably, take some limited action against Serbia, but it could hardly spread into a general war.

For the *Cormoran* this lack of genuine concern about possible war was of crucial significance. She was laid up in drydock undergoing major overhaul. In accordance with long-standing practice, the responsible crews had carefully dismantled her engine and spread the various parts throughout the modern workshops of Tsingtao. They had, as well, unloaded all ammunition and supplies into the warehouses along the waterfront. The ship, empty and stripped of her power, remained little more than a hollow metal shell.

During the extensive overhaul the ship's crew enjoyed the pleasures of the port with scarcely a thought of the future. After their long voyage through the protectorates and their collective bout with malaria, they were delighted to while away the time playing games on the beach, drinking beer in the many taverns, and exchanging wild sea-tales with the colorful naval people always present in the city. The weather was glorious and the quietude a magnificent cure for all ailments—real and imaginary. In sum, the sailors congratulated themselves upon their good fortune.

Tsingtao was not home but it provided an adequate substitute for the dreamed reality of the homeland. Unfortunately this period of sensual pleasure did not have a long existence. On July 7 orders from Berlin canceled the long-planned movement of the cruiser *Emden* to the Yangtze River. With von Spee and the other fleet units all at sea, she was the sole German warship of any consequence in the entire area. Shortly afterward all the lesser naval units in Chinese waters received instructions to move toward the port. The German merchantmen, scattered throughout the world, likewise had warnings that they should seek German or neutral harbors, that is, ports not under the authority of the possible belligerents. The small river gunboats, *Vaterland*, *Tsingtao*, and *Otter*, simply disarmed on the Yangtze, and their crews hurried to Tsingtao by whatever means they could find, for reassignment.

On July 22 the old Austrian cruiser *Kaiserin-Elisabeth* (finished in 1890 with a displacement of 4,060 tons, eight 6-inch guns, and a speed of twenty knots) appeared off the harbor entrance and asked permission to enter. Her unannounced visit shocked the residents into concerned activity. The threat of war was very real now; the Austrian had not come for a surprise courtesy call. She was seeking a friendly haven beyond the grasp of Russian fleet units.

While the newcomer received a warm welcome and prompt social exchanges soon created an excellent rapport between the various ship's crews, the immediate concern remained politics. They could discuss few topics beyond the uncertain outcomes of events transpiring on the other side of the globe. The ship's parties now had a constant patriotic theme, with much display of flags and singing of national songs. At every one of them, however, at least one person was always delegated to keep watch for wireless news about European events.

As the *Kaiserin-Elisabeth*'s crew gradually entered into the hospitality games, the face of Tsingtao altered its complexion a good deal. The port filled with an ever-increasing number of vessels, most of them small coastal steamers running from individual insecurity toward collective confidence in the German port. On the whole they were a shabby lot, unkempt, with multiple scars of long service in the difficult waters of Asia. Their military usefulness was, beyond their experienced manpower, sorely limited. In the city, dozens of reservists appeared from stange-sounding places, often in equally unusual garb. They had long since disposed of all uniforms and official connection with the service. Nonetheless they reported back when the long naval administrative arm reached them with unexpected and impatient orders. The tempo of harbor life increased its beat. War's possible onset provided the motive force needed to move men to extended effort.

Among the more concerned persons was the captain of the *Cormoran*, Adalbert Zuckschwerdt, a large, handsome, mountainous man with wide, muscular shoulders, and a decisive personality. Rather than patiently explore a problem to its exhausted depths, he normally chose action and prompt decision making. He was an ingratiating figure, known to virtually everyone among the naval units in the Far East. By temperament a quiet man, he seldom raised his voice, never used profanity, and avoided harsh exchanges at all costs. This quiet demeanor concealed a streak of innate stubbornness, which he camouflaged with a social consciousness not often found in either the German navy or among westerners in the Far East. His quick wit, sincere concern for others, and easy manner made him a popular figure everywhere. He had been in the Orient for almost four years and had established an enviable reputation for fairness and discipline.

Although as late in awakening to the threat of war as anyone else, Zuckschwerdt reacted with far greater strength and dispatch. He realized that war was bound to threaten both himself and his crew with its unpleasant possibilities and quite probable capture and imprisonment. His vessel was obviously too old and possessed too limited a range to be an effective warship. Her voracious appetite for coal precluded even limited punitive expeditions. Nonetheless there was no replacement; she would have to do.

On the day following the *Kaiserin-Elisabeth*'s arrival, Zuckschwerdt ordered the immediate acceleration of repair work. He insisted upon round-the-clock activity and used all his excess manpower to shift ammunition, supplies, and other materials into warehouses for prompt, efficient loading once the ship was seaworthy. There were no complaints by the German sailors over labor normally performed by Chinese coolies. In the middle of this frenetic activity the senior officer in Tsingtao, Capt. Karl von Muller, commander of the cruiser *Emden*, received a communique from Berlin revealing the serious nature of the crisis. He immediately called all the local ship's captains together for a lengthy council on the following morning. They discussed the deteriorating political situation and agreed 1) to continue the all-out effort to repair the *Cormoran*, 2) to hasten the departure of all colliers out of the base, 3) to prepare the city for siege, and 4) to shift personnel to various other cities in order to coordinate subsequent operations.

That same afternoon a further message from the Berlin admiralty staff reached Tsingtao with a detailed report on the increasing political tension. The Russians were mobilizing, and there did not appear to be any way to avoid war. There was, unfortunately for the Tsingtao observers, no way to know which nations would be enemies in this conflict. Muller considered his position and the instructions he had received from Admiral von Spee before the latter's departure. The senior commander had suggested that, in the event of major war, the Tsingtao squadron should protect its base as well as other German colonies, provide colliers at strategic points for further operations, and avoid being caught in home port and blockaded. Muller, an impetuous, venturesome soul, chose to anticipate events rather than permit history to catch him asleep.

He ordered the *Emden* prepared for sea and the possibility of cruiser warfare. His crew began the difficult task of removing all items not required for military action. All excess clothing, unnecessary furniture, and the souvenirs collected during many voyages had to be set ashore on the most limited notice. Likewise Muller wanted all carpets, curtains, wooden furnishings, anything liable to burn or splinter, set aside. As the flow of materials off the ship reached a steady, acceptable pace, it encountered an equal bulk coming the other way. The ammunition, coal, and foodstuffs for a lengthy voyage eventually filled every storage corner. Whatever was left over had to be put on deck and tied down. Within a short time, the *Emden*, normally a model of ordered cleanliness, became a moving junk ship filled to overflowing with interesting wares. In the center of these two lines of constantly moving humans stood Muller, shouting commands while joking with his charges as they hurried by on their assigned chores.

As Muller directed the ship's preparations, he discussed his position with an impatient Zuckschwerdt. Given the war plans and the concurrent diplomatic situation, Muller had decided to take the *Emden* to sea. Under these circumstances Zuckschwerdt would become the ranking naval commander in Tsingtao. The two men went over the issues and problems while seated between the two continuously moving human chains. Once they had completed their conversation, Zuckschwerdt shook hands, wished Muller a good trip, and reluctantly returned, with a slow step, to his landlocked command. Muller turned to his crew and pushed them through the night. At seven o'clock on July 31 the emotionally charged sailors cast off the *Emden*'s mooring lines and the cruiser moved out into the Yellow Sea.

As she eased down the harbor approaches Muller watched his advance ship, the torpedo boat *S-90* for intelligence on the possible presence of foreign warships outside the harbor. There were none. Nonetheless Muller ordered "Action stations" as soon as the *Emden* reached the open sea. While there was no enemy vessel in sight, the captain wanted to keep his men alert and concerned with every possibility. Late in the night of August 1 the ship's wireless operator brought the awaited news of war with Russia. The following day was Sunday, but the radio report appreciably altered the day's routine. Muller turned all hands to the final preparation for action—ammunition conversion, combat drill, and another search of the ship for unneeded combustibles. After these assignments had been completed to the captain's satisfaction, everyone attended divine services. Following the solemn religious ceremony, and a brief address to the ship's complement, Muller turned his ship toward Tsushima Straits. He had an enemy and hoped to find Russian shipping along the Nagasaki-Vladivostok trade lane.

On August 4 his aggressive efforts brought success. The *Emden*'s lookouts reported smoke on the horizon, and Muller ordered an immediate chase. Cutting through a hard-rolling sea, the *Emden*, with all power extended, closed the distance separating her from the quarry responsible for the black cloud. As the *Emden* moved closer Muller himself could see that she was a fast Russian passenger ship. When the *Emden* fired a warning shot, the steamer instantly began evasive action while sending out a wild melange of incoherent wireless messages. Muller had no desire to lose his find nor to allow her time to send out proper notice of the clash and its location. He brought several guns to bear and fired a few rounds, the last one passing through the Russian ship's rigging.

The closeness of the final shell persuaded the Russian captain of the certain futility of further resistance and he promptly brought his ship about in a heart-frightening turn and stopped, all the while giving out a steady S.O.S. The *Emden*, guns loaded for a single, destructive broadside, slowly breasted the Russian while trying to jam the enemy's persistent and now dangerous wireless activity. Within a few minutes Muller knew his prize. She was the *Rjasan*, and the crew quickly struck her flag, to preclude any misunderstood intentions. Muller was pleased to note that she was a passenger-merchantman constructed in Germany in 1909, with a respectable speed of some fourteen knots.

Without delay Muller sent off a prize crew under Lt. Julius Lauterbach. In a brief, hurried discussion just as the latter was about to shift vessels, they agreed to take the *Rjasan* back to Tsingtao, with the idea of converting her into an auxiliary cruiser. The rotund Lauterbach almost did not made his new command, when the small boat put down by the *Emden* just missed crashing against the cruiser's stern in a heavy swell. Once aboard the Russian vessel, he quickly established control and brought his new command into line behind Muller. He found the *Rjasan* carrying tea, salt meat, spirits, and iron rails, in addition to a few passengers. Also Lauterbach evaluated the captive vessel. She was an adequate 3,400 gross tons. Her spacious quarters could accommodate 400 men, which made her a valuable prize. Lauterbach communicated his hasty evaluation to Muller, who confirmed his earlier decision to take her back to Tsingtao for German use. The *Emden* turned home with the first German naval prize of the First World War. It was a prideful moment for everyone aboard the victor.

En route to Tsingtao they encountered various Japanese vessels and heard, through the busy wireless, about Great Britain's entrance into the conflict. All around them came the radio noise of ship's wirelesses—some of the vessels were obviously very close. Rather than risk any engagement with a heavier enemy warship, Muller remained directly on his homeward course. He was fortunate, and there were no confrontations to interrupt or mar the *Emden*'s glory. Flushed with success, Muller shepherded his prize into the harbor to the enthusiastic cheers of the sailors still in the city.

As the *Emden* reached the coaling docks where previously alerted labor gangs stood ready for their assignments, many persons hurried on board to congratulate Muller. In the van was Zuckschwerdt, who elbowed his colleagues out of the way in a fashion well outside the customary etiquette of the German navy and his own correct personal manners. He was on a far more selfish and, thereby, more important mission than mere congratulations. Muller turned such sentiments, including Zuckschwerdt's, brusquely aside and ordered his first officer to supervise the refueling process. Then, having given precise instructions for the immediate future, Muller hurried off for his duty report to the German governor, Alfred Meyer-Waldeck. As he left the ship Muller motioned Zuckschwerdt to accompany him so that they could discuss matters of mutual interest en route.

Although the dilapidated automobile at their disposal impeded their conversation with its frightening, clanking vibrations, Zuckschwerdt dutifully informed his superior about the changes in Tsingtao since the *Emden*'s departure. He had decided to place the former luxury passenger ship *Prinz Eitel Friedrich* into commission as a merchant raider manned by the crews of the old gunboats, *Tiger* and *Luchs*. The commander of the latter, Capt. Max Thierichens, was to assume command of the former pleasure cruiser. Zuckschwerdt had also taken the time to organize the city's defenses and military chains of command. With sailors from all over the Orient in port, there were not enough ships to use them. Those unable to find a normal berth had to be trained as infantry soldiers, an occupation for which they were ill-prepared by experience and for which they were ill-suited by temperament.

Finally Zuckschwerdt turned to the most significant matter, one of intense personal concern. The *Cormoran*'s crew, laboring frantically day and night with the dock workers, had reassembled the ship's engine on August 5. Zuckschwerdt had immediately ordered a test run in the harbor. It had ended in total disaster. The speed of repair resulted in poor quality control in the workmanship. As the ship got underway, her engine could not stand the pressures and began to cast off parts with the agonizing jerky motion of a snake shedding its skin. Because of this jarring motion, with its uneven thrust, the *Cormoran*'s propeller shaft gave way. Instead of the anticipated success, the ship had ingloriously returned to the dockyard with the help of several lesser boats. Repairs would demand several more days, and Zuckschwerdt feared that the expansion of the war to the Far East might not allow the necessary time. Just as his morale had fallen to the edge of depression, the news of the *Emden*'s victory had reached the city. For Zuckschwerdt the report proffered some hope.

He explained to the impatient Muller, who listened while exhorting the driver to greater haste, the import of the *Rjasan*'s capture to German naval activity. The entire crew of the *Cormoran* had, without formal command, appeared at the dock to greet the *Emden*'s triumphal return with welcoming cheers. Their shouts, surely the loudest of the celebrants, were for hope for themselves as well as congratulations for the *Emden*'s success. They agreed that the Russian made a good visual impression. She had a low upper deck, running in a direct line from bow to stern, with two stumpy funnels marring the midship arrangement. Her design inspired confidence in both her speed and maneuverability. The newcomer could clearly travel, in contrast to the sadly crippled old *Cormoran*.

Muller responded tersely to the report, congratulating Zuckschwerdt's powers of observation concerning the captive Russian. He stated that the *Rjasan* had been constructed in Elbing, Germany by the respectable Schickau firm, was five years old, displaced some 5,100 tons, and could make fourteen knots. She was a member of the Russian Volunteer Fleet, which indicated a possible Russian disposition to convert her into an auxiliary cruiser during wartime. Zuckschwerdt, unable to contain himself, interrupted his superior's measured speech and asked Muller for permission to convert the prize into a German raider.

Just as he finished his emotional appeal, the automobile halted at the governor's house. Muller, fully aware of the unanswered query, hurried inside with Zuckschwerdt in close pursuit. Without response to his colleague, Muller reported to Meyer-Waldeck about his voyage. He also informed the governor that the *Emden* would leave for von Spee's squadron as soon as the first officer completed loading the food and fuel supplies. After this brief summary Muller finally addressed himself to the *Rjasan* issue. He informed both listeners of his earlier decision to convert her into a warship and asked permission to assign Zuckschwerdt the command and the supervision of her reconstruction. The governor agreed to the proposal without demur.

The ecstatic Zuckschwerdt, avoiding any thought about Muller's exasperating sense of humor, excused himself from his superior as soon as they left the governor's House and hurried back to the dock area alone. He immediately went on board the Russian vessel for a rapid inspection preparatory to converting the vessel to wartime use. The Russian captain, who spoke fluent German, was still aboard and asked Zuckschwerdt's help in contacting his home office by wireless. Zuckschwerdt refused because of the war. The Russian then asked for permission to visit the local Russian consulate.

The German responded that the Russians did not have their own consul, but that they had hired a German long before the outbreak of hostilities for this function. Since the war's beginning that dignitary, a Bavarian reserve officer, had been activated and his obligations to the tsar had been terminated with a brief explanatory message. Beyond that, the individual involved hoped to serve Germany on the *Rjasan* as soon as she was converted into a German naval vessel. This final declaration was too much for the harried captive officer, who completely lost his temper. In a wild rage he cursed the barbaric Germans, the entire concept and practice of war, and the cruel fates which had conspired to bring him to Tsingtao. Zuckschwerdt, both taken aback and somewhat frightened by the display, called for assistance. Ultimately several crewmen were required to subdue the unruly Russian captain and to escort him off his own ship into captivity.

His emotional outburst created sympathy among the Germans but no support; they had their own concerns. For them the *Rjasan* was the means for their deliverance from an undesirable position as potential infantrymen. After his inspection, Zuckschwerdt supervised the movement of the *Rjasan* to the dock adjacent to the disabled *Cormoran*. He brought her into position at one o'clock that same afternoon. For the nearby German crew, crowded like uncertain flies on a dying animal, the new neighbor proved the efficacy of fervent prayer. The new arrival might save them. Her cargo of iron rails, wine, lemons, and salted meat required only minimal unloading. Most of it could be used later with little adjustment.

Beyond the cargo manifests, however, there were serious obstacles to switching identities and reequipping the newest recruit for service in the Asiatic squadron. To begin with, she was in an atrocious state of repair. The filth piled up throughout the ship reflected months of inattention and lack of concern for even nominal maintenance standards. Following a careful cleaning, the Germans began the conversion from civilian status to military preparedness. While the Russian naval manuals, including those aboard the ship, clearly listed the *Rjasan* as part of their merchant marine earmarked for wartime military activity, they found numerous difficulties in the assigned task.

The translation of instrument designations, adjustment of equipment in accordance with German standards, and location of significant points for repair and maintenance work appeared to be problems easy of resolution, but the sailors called upon to execute them remained less than enthusiastic. Such matters demanded not only resolute and immediate decisions but also much thought and consideration. But there was time for neither. Zuckschwerdt refused to countenance any obstructions, and his men quickly learned to avoid him with such concerns. He seldom left the ship as he drove his crew through twelve-hour shifts—dividing the work in such fashion that the night force could function properly under the huge lights illuminating the area. His injunctions to hurry were really quite superfluous. While the captain's presence was a direct, continuous influence (he slept on his new command only for a few minutes at a time), the thought of long isolation in Tsingtao and probable imprisonment somewhere else provided an indirect psychological impetus of major proportion. Also in the middle of these intense activities Zuckschwerdt was required to interrupt his supervising role twice, but he was not pleased over either interference with his task.

The first interruption was on the morning of August 7, when he led a flag parade to commission the new merchant raider. She carried the name *Cormoran*. In part this was a tribute to her namesake's years of diligent and uncomplaining service. Even more significant, however, the name provided a useful intelligence ploy. Should the western powers occupy Tsingtao, as seemed inevitable, the original *Cormoran* would be scuttled, leaving the impression that she had expired without progeny. In celebrating the victory the allies might overlook the captured *Rjasan* and neglect to search for the newly designated namesake.

The other break was for the farewell ceremonies for the *Emden*. Muller took his leave that same afternoon and, promptly, at four o'clock cast off the final restraining line. He much preferred the uncertainties of the open sea to Tsingtao's confining shores. Zuckschwerdt was of like mind.

Within four days of her arrival Zuckschwerdt had the new *Cormoran* ready for sea duty. In that brief time he had supervised the movement and placement of eight 4-inch guns and two floodlights. All ammunition, provisions for a five-month voyage, and over 2,000 tons of coal rested in various recesses of the ship. The earlier preparations in the warehouses paid a handsome reward, as the loading moved forward without a single untoward interruption.

The fuel problem was the most serious concern. In view of her limited operational range, the old *Rjasan* had bunker space for a mere 350 tons of coal, which was far too limited for the German military requirements. Obviously Zuckschwerdt had a simple solution for this unacceptable situation: he chose to fill every available container with the black chunks necessary for existence in an enemy-controlled sea. He ordered most of the living quarters, cargo holds, recreation areas, and all dead space converted into coal bins. The crew would simply have to live on deck. Since, in the tropics most crewmen spent most of their time outside anyway, the requirement would not be a harsh one. During bad weather there would be complaints, but Zuckschwerdt decided that survival had to rule over comfort. With 2,500 tons of coal he could cruise for 10,000 miles without refueling.

The crew selection was no easier. During the previous June replacements from Germany had, in accordance with regular naval practice, reached Tsingtao and replaced one quarter of the old *Cormoran*'s crew. These men had not really had sufficient time for mastering their new assignments. They could not know the required order, teamwork, or spirit of the ship. With limited naval service for the most part, these men had to learn through the drills and other experiences aboard ship. While this money-saving training device served a practical peacetime function, it did not provide a truly operative crew, particularly at the time of changeover. The war caught the *Cormoran* in a vulnerable position. While the other units of the German squadron in the Orient suffered from the same problem, they had had a brief time, in contrast to the *Cormoran*, to partially assimilate the newcomers. After a brief, but thoughtful delay Zuckschwerdt decided in favor of keeping his recruits, assuming that their enthusiasm would bring ability in short order. In addition he selected volunteers from the old gunboats, *Iltis* and *Vaterland*, as well as a few specialized experts from the local reservists.

Since the *Cormoran* promised to be the last vessel out of Tsingtao, there were few non-volunteers, and the selection process was not only for a difficult and uncertain undertaking for those who won but an almost certain prison sentence for those who lost. The pressures were manifestly intense, and those selected to remain behind presented a sorry appearance. In sum Zuckschwerdt had 24 officers, 218 men, and 15 helpers. These latter included 11 New Guinea youths recruited for miscellaneous requirements aboard ship, and 4 Chinese laundrymen. The captain informed each one of the helpers that the ship might be in some danger, but each one responded in the curious Tsingtao pidgin German, "Jetzt Krieg sein; Colmolan plenty bumbum machemachei Ihr Taitai vielleicht nicht wiedersehen! Maski! Wir plenty cash machemache!" ("Now war be comin comin *Cormoran* plenty boom boom, make make. Your wife might not see again. Of no matter, we plenty cash money make make!") The adventurous spirit, escape possibilities, and prospective rewards provided sufficient inducements. *Cormoran* had a crew.

Zuckschwerdt had precious little time to consider either the strange humor or the tragic possibilities of his situation. On August 8 he learned that the Japanese fleet, under sealed orders, had left its home port, Sasebo, for an unknown destination. The following day a Berlin telegram reported that Japan would soon attack Tsingtao, and the home authorities ordered the garrison to full alert. This announcement was sufficiently disturbing for Zuckschwerdt to accelerate his departure. He ordered the *Cormoran* to sea on August 10.

She had not had even a trial run with her new crew. Her engines, beyond a superficial investigation of the boiler and visible working parts, had not been properly inspected, and her loading, carried on under chaotic pressures, had not been tested in any way. The crew, each member desperately concerned for his personal safety, had barely had time to exchange names. Despite all these patent inadequacies, Zuckschwerdt decided to chance everything, for the ever-increasing Japanese wireless traffic augured ill for the immediate future. He worked everyone until noon on August 10 and then ordered an unexpected halt. Those projects still unfinished at that moment were abandoned. Among them Zuckschwerdt felt remorse over two—the animal pen had to be omitted and the ice machine, which the Russians had let deteriorate, had to be left unrepaired.

After a brief speech Zuckschwerdt ordered the mooring lines cast off, and at 2:00 P.M. the *Cormoran* edged away from the crowded pier. Many old friends were present for a last "Auf Wiedersehen." The separation was not like many past departures. Everyone realized that it would be many months before they might meet again; perhaps never. The *Cormoran*, an untried vessel with an untried crew was departing into the unknown while those remaining faced certain siege by overwhelming enemy forces. They joined, therefore, in the songs which meant so much to Germans, "Wacht am Rhein" and "Lieb Vaterland magst ruhig sein." With a heavy flow of tears on both sides of the widening stretch of water, the *Cormoran* departed for the harbor entrance.

The last visual communication was a flag signal from the governor extending his best wishes for a successful campaign. In accordance with Zuckschwerdt's specific orders, every available man in the area had a last look at the comforting sight of Tsingtao with the neat, orderly houses resting in front of the green hills. Then the captain issued the order, "Look forward." The mental image of past pleasures and peaceful activities was broken. From the comforts of a former era of peaceful somnolence a simple about-face revealed a new horizon—the ugly, misshapen figure of war. The *Cormoran* had to contemplate the inevitable confrontation with the foe.

Outside the immediate harbor the torpedo boat *S-90*, which had left some two hours earlier as an advance scout, reported that the horizon was clear. There was no enemy vessel in sight nor within hearing, and the *Cormoran* made the open, now unfriendly, sea.

During the night the authorities in Tsingtao informed Zuckschwerdt that, according to various newspaper accounts, the

VOYAGE of the CORMORAN 1914

0 — 1000
MILES at EQUATOR

PACIFIC

OCEAN

JAPAN

Japan

Sea

MARIANA
IS

Guam

Yap

CAROLINE IS.

MARSHALL
IS

Jaluit

New
Guinea

KAISER W. LAND

Friedrich W.
Harbor

SOLOMON
IS

GILBERT
IS

ELLICE
IS

Sea

Coral Sea

NEW
HEBRIDES

FIJI IS

New
Caledonia

ALIA

150   165   180
45

30

23.5

15

0

15

23.5

150   165   180

P. G. R - 1978

Japanese cruiser *Tone*, with four torpedo boats, was en route to stations somewhere in the South Pacific. Six other cruisers and eleven torpedo boats were feverishly completing preparations to leave their home port of Sasebo. The English consul in Tsingtao, who was just completing preparations for his final departure, had received news of a Japanese ultimatum to Germany. Given these details, Zuckschwerdt decided against immediate operations in the Tsingtao area. He wanted his ship out of the confining Yellow Sea as rapidly as possible. The collection of major naval units moving in, through, and about that area precluded aggressive activity by so small a vessel. He decided to move rapidly southward in order to pass through the islands between Japan and Formosa. These insular links effectively blocked egress from north to south. Beyond that land chain there were some active trade routes and no immediate threat from enemy warships. En route to that free area, however, the *Cormoran* had to cross the crowded traffic lane, Japan-Shanghai-Hong Kong, and the equally dangerous zone opposite the mouth of the Yangtze River.

On August 11, as the *Cormoran* moved past the river, the weather provided excellent cover. Thick dark clouds obscured the sky, while equally heavy fog belts hindered all direct vision. Working through this welcome natural protection, the *Cormoran* did not sight the smoke trail of a single vessel. The same weather conditions prevailed the following day, although two small Japanese coastal ships put in an unwelcome appearance and brought the crew to watchful attention. Zuckschwerdt broke out the Russian flag and moved slowly away—seemingly the harmless *Rjasan*. That evening the lookouts announced that Tori Island in the Ryukyus was on the horizon. Zuckschwerdt wanted to slip through these islands by ten o'clock to avoid land observation or local fishing vessels and to allow as much movement as possible into the ocean beyond under the protective cover of darkness. As the *Cormoran* began its dash through the blackness, there was a sudden increase in wireless activity around the vessel.

The news was not overly surprising, in view of the earlier revelations from Tsingtao concerning Japanese fleet movements. What was disconcerting was the volume and clarity of the exchanges, which indicated a most unpleasant proximity. Zuckschwerdt assumed that the *Tone*, with her accompanying torpedo boats, was responsible for the noise, and he desperately wanted to avoid any chance encounter. He was still uncertain about Japan's status in the war and feared a meeting with that nation's naval units. At first he thought that the all-encompassing darkness of night would cover his activity, but this hope lasted little more than an hour. A most unwanted brilliant moon appeared over a clear sea and provided, in addition to romantic illumination of the ship, a superlative view of the horizon. There was no alternative and the captain ordered full speed ahead. The engines soon hummed with the roar of machinery driven to full capacity. Everyone listened for the first false note in the mechanical rhythm, because this was the initial effort to drive the vessel so hard.

In between the cacophony of moving metal were the crackling sounds, in unweakened intensity, of the Japanese wirelesses. With the continued emotional stress imposed by this noise, no one noticed an appreciable change in the sea around them. Eventually Lt. Hans Muller, one of the ship's officers on board, answered a call of nature. On the way back to his post he noted the increased salt spray cast up by the waves rolling behind the *Cormoran*. They were far higher and more unruly than he remembered them from earlier observations. He reported this change to the captain.

Zuckschwerdt immediately noted the correctness of the report as well as its implication. The sea had indeed grown much stronger; to a point where it was running too high for torpedo boats. He then remembered that the previous afternoon a Chinese radio station had issued a general warning against an imminent typhoon some distance from the *Cormoran*. The excitement of the moment had caused the station to neglect important details. In all probability the Japanese had heard the same report and had taken refuge in a small, protected bay. Such action would account for the intensity and clarity of their wireless activity. Zuckschwerdt expressed the fervent wish that his ship had a peaceful harbor where he could spend a restful night—a desire echoed by everyone within earshot of his plea. But by midnight the ship had cleared the islands and the crew was free to enjoy the glorious moon reflected in the water. The engaging sight of fast-moving swells tossing their foam-covered tops into the moon's reflective beams was again one of the sea's attractions. Even a communique from Tsingtao, reporting that the Japanese had mobilized their fleet and would soon move out to hunt German shipping, failed to disturb the unique setting. It was a moment for solemn thought, not to be disturbed by petty immediate concerns. The instant passed, however, and more realistic matters occupied everyone. Although the ship had evaded action in the confined northern Pacific and set course for the southern regions, she still had a vast amount of water to pass over. Yet, nonetheless, the crew was now far more confident about its possible future. The crewmen had the prospect of seeing their friends in the cruiser squadron once more and the abiding comfort that the *Cormoran* had survived her first real test. The continuing throb of her engines gave noisy testimony to her strength. Zuckschwerdt, whose internal confidence now equaled that of an earlier false exterior, issued new orders for the Marianas.

In doing so he was somewhat concerned about the silence of the German radio station on Yap. Despite its limited size, the island held an all-important position in the German communications network. It controlled the two cables of the German-Dutch Telegraph Company from Menado (in the Celebes Islands) and Shanghai. Moreover there was a connecting link, via Guam, to the great Pacific cable, San Francisco-Manila. Since the total silence indicated possible Allied destruction, Zuckschwerdt had to consider the importance of this loss. The end of Yap's communication station would not bother him momentarily because Tsingtao wireless facilities had sufficient power to reach the *Cormoran*. He could not, however, assume that Tsingtao would be able to transmit indefinitely. To use his own wireless was obviously dangerous, because enemy vessels could approximate his position within a brief time and take appropriate action. Nonetheless Zuckschwerdt, weighing all the alternatives, decided on August 14 that his ship was sufficiently distant from probable enemy units to make a modest test of his wireless in a search for friends.

The first call received a prompt response from the German steamer *Ahlers*, some eighty sea miles away. Her wireless reporter relayed in addition to her location the interesting news that the ship's lookouts could see an English steamer on the horizon. Zuckschwerdt promptly altered his course and prepared for action. The gun crews practiced their firing techniques with profound care once more (the guns had not yet been fired from their new positions), and a boarding party prepared for action against the enemy. Zuckschwerdt went so far as to select a prize crew for his envisaged captive. But, in the midst of these activities the *Ahlers* broke wireless silence to state that the earlier observation had been erroneous. The vessel in question was really the North-German Lloyd steamer, *Göttingen*, which did not possess a wireless. In addition, her wily captain had altered her appearance following the declaration of war, occasioning the mistaken identity. The *Ahlers* suggested, therefore, that the *Cormoran's* presence was no longer needed in the area. Zuckschwerdt turned back on his earlier course, disappointed with the fates which had denied him his first action.

That evening the *Cormoran's* wireless operators raised the *Scharnhorst*, flagship of Admiral Graf von Spee. The latter, acting with promptness famous throughout Asia, ordered the *Cormoran* to convoy the *Ahlers* and *Göttingen* to the cruiser squadron in the Marshall Islands. He chose the less desirable but more isolated anchorage at Majuro for the rendezvous. For von Spee the meeting was of utmost significance. He was unable to hear any German wireless stations and was isolated from the rest of the world and fast-moving current events. He desperately needed immediate information about Germany's circumstances in the expanding conflict.

While the instructions were clear, their execution was not so easily accomplished. On August 16 the rapid fall of the barometer heralded the arrival of the typhoon whose threat had helped the *Cormoran* through the Japanese islands. By afternoon the mounting waves, dark clouds, and high winds provided ample evidence of the storm's severity and the *Cormoran's* proximity to its center. There was no way to run from the raw weather certain to lie directly ahead. By evening great walls of water crashed over the ship, giving many concerned souls on board fearful doubts about the propriety of volunteering for sea duty. The Chinese laundrymen began hurried preparations for their burial at sea, which gave little comfort to their frightened comrades. The *Cormoran* shuddered and shook under the crushing blows of the sea, but she always came up again, albeit often after considerable deliberation, to meet the next challenge. Her reaction time was slow because she lay deep in the water under the weight of the burdensome coal supply. The vessel righted herself, nonetheless, and proved the excellence of her original design. In fact, she actually had fewer problems in the boiling water than did the crew which had precious few moments to admire nature's powerful handiwork.

The scenes around the ship would have occasioned amused laughter under quieter circumstances. There were many comic cameo parts played by every member of the ship's crew. The ship's gunnery officer was the first to unwillingly engage in this humorous sporting activity, when various ammunition boxes broke loose from their ropes. They had been fastened down properly in Tsingtao, but the water's steady pounding soon wore through their moorings. As the poor officer and his aides tied down a few heavy crates in one place, another pile would begin sliding across the deck to threaten life and limb. Like termites fighting a flood they ran from one point to another in continual danger, as the water constantly broke over them and then rolled along the ship's deck in varying depths.

On the forward deck, the executive officer, Lt. Hans Muller, and a group of sailors desperately fought to catch a small boat which had broken loose from its moorings. The frantic sailors caught the broken lines but could not control their quarry. As it moved from one side of the ship to the other, they shifted with it, unable to gain control but equally unwilling to surrender. In the end they had to give way to exhaustion, and the tiny boat went over the side as the *Cormoran*'s sacrifice to the sea gods.

The radio personnel had an equally difficult time with their responsibilities. Almost immediately the typhoon winds broke the all-important aerial wires, which whipped in the air like errant fishing lines. Since there was no immediate prospect of meeting a repair ship, the operators had to save as much wire as possible. Presenting a grotesque ballet spectacle, they desperately ran between the waterfalls cascading down around them, grappling for the wildly blowing metal strands. Had it not been so deadly serious, the humor of the situation would have created a cabaret atmosphere for the enjoyment of all concerned.

The men, with few exceptions due to total exhaustion, maintained their morale throughout the struggle. They were in the open air and, although soaked to the skin from the incessant hail and rain, warm from the humid tropical temperatures. Activity precluded depression. Far more serious was the state of the ship's stores. In view of the long voyage with its concomitant fuel requirements, Zuckschwerdt had risked placing his provisions in a number of makeshift areas below deck. These temporary closets and shelves were in no way adequate for the stress imposed by the typhoon and gave way almost immediately under the pressures. There followed a wild rolling back and forth of large numbers of bottles, boxes, cans, and miscellaneous goods, in which the breakage, particularly of beer bottles, was very high. The crew members sent to control the battle of the supplies faced a severe task in controlling the moving chaos. All the hatches were closed against the elements while the ship rocked crazily back and forth, pitching in every direction of the compass. The mixture of unknown smells and the lack of air circulation created a volatile, atmospheric quality which made many sailors violently ill. Their friends had to help them outside, removing needed assistance with the work at hand. Within a short time the sloshing mess had created a real shambles. The battle went on, hour after hour.

Finally, after eighteen hours of constant struggle the crew noted a gradual change in the wind, and the barometric pressure slowly edged its way upward. The ship had survived a major ordeal with great success.

The following evening everyone participated in a pleasant meal while exchanging personal experiences of the storm. Certainly they had been through an exciting adventure and escaped with only a few human bruises and irritating, albeit minor, ship's damage. On the other hand they had taken some of the sea's hardest blows and knew the staying power of their ship. There was a spirit of camaraderie born from the action which welded the unusual assemblage of Tsingtao into a prideful crew. It was a good omen.

The cooks served early breakfast on August 18 under two magnificent stars which managed to break through the otherwise oppressive, low-hanging clouds. Beyond heralding a break in the weather, they served to help fix the *Cormoran*'s position. She had been driven well off course, about one hundred sea miles west of the Marianas Islands. Because of the continuing rains and high seas, the lookouts could not see the horizon, and Zuckschwerdt feared the possibility of hitting one of the crater islands which abounded in the area. Navigating with extreme caution, the *Cormoran* managed to ride the swells left over from the typhoon and moved around the islands.

Zuckschwerdt could now return to his assigned mission. The

Göttingen and *Ahlers* had been north of the *Cormoran* and had missed most of the storm's force. After contacting the latter vessel by wireless, Zuckschwerdt established a contact point, and all three vessels hurried toward it. En route Zuckschwerdt put his crew to work cleaning up the mess left from one storm. Although he disliked the risk of announcing his presence to the enemy, he had to permit the disposal of considerable refuse. For many hours the ship's wake was colored with litter as the crew cleaned up the storm's destruction. As the *Cormoran* moved happily along once more, the ship's radiomen once more heard from Tsingtao, where the authorities revealed the ominous news of the Japanese ultimatum to Germany and the certainty of war.

Given this new addition to the enemy, Zuckschwerdt renewed his efforts to train his crew for the hardships he anticipated in the conflict ahead. Once the ship was clean, he forbade garbage disposal which would reveal the *Cormoran*'s presence to the enemy. He ordered double watches to maintain proper diligence and collective alertness. He also instituted surprise training drills day and night often at strange hours. These efforts received his personal attention, and he was careful to time every group. For those who failed to meet his demanding standards, there were harsh words and extra-duty training hours. He earned the respect of his crew through these activities because he was always present himself rather than delegating the job to a subordinate.

On August 21 the *Cormoran* met its two charges and started the small convoy toward the cruiser squadron. The meeting was most welcome to Zuckschwerdt's crew, because the *Göttingen* had an extensive accumulation of livestock on board, and the animals had not weathered the storm in good condition. For the *Cormoran*'s complement this misfortune brought fresh meat, a welcome change from the heavily salted, preserved beef that they had been eating for some time. The *Göttingen* also had a fine supply of beer to wash down the meat and help the crew's morale.

In the morning of August 25 the trio encountered the former Chinese coastal steamer, *Gouverneur Jaschke*, which had just been released by Admiral von Spee. Her captain informed them that they were very close to the cruiser squadron. With this preliminary assurance that all was well ahead of them the tiny convoy hurried on. Two days later the ships pushed slowly into the lagoon of Majuro Island. Behind the many palm trees towering high into the air at the entrance reef, they could see the masts of many vessels. The *Cormoran*, as the senior vessel, led the way into the lagoon, but with measured caution. Like so many Pacific islands the large, circular basin had been formed by reefs which created natural protection for all vessels anchored inside. Since few of these reefs had been charted they posed immediate and serious challenges to the unwary sailor.

After carefully picking their way through the coral maze, Zuckschwerdt's force received a totally unexpected emotional reception. From over a thousand throats the latecomers heard "Hurrah, Hurrah, Hurrah!" This massive welcome was followed by the unison singing of "Lieb Vaterland magst ruhig sein." Were it not for the war, the martial meeting would surely have been a splendid pleasure affair of impressive proportions. As it was, the crews of the three vessels entering the harbor stood along the rails, waving to the enthusiastic sailors aboard the cruisers *Scharnhorst* and *Gneisenau*, the auxiliary cruiser, *Prinz Eitel Friedrich*, and the merchantmen, *Titania*, *Yorck*, *Prinz Waldemar*, *Holsatia*, *Mark*, and *Longman*. The light cruisers of the squadron were away on other missions. Spee had sent the *Nürnberg* off to Honolulu with telegrams; the *Emden* was someplace in the Indian Ocean; and the *Leipzig* was scouting along the South American coast. Even as the loud greetings faded away, the sounds of intense activity replaced them. Time was far too valuable for lengthy exchange, no matter how close the friendship. The lagoon was the scene of universal activity as the merchantmen passed materials to the heavier war vessels. Back and forth moved the ungainly ship's boats, tiny shells on a clear blue sea ferrying their cargoes along every ray of the compass.

Zuckschwerdt, much impressed with the sight, hurried aboard the *Scharnhorst* and reported to Admiral von Spee. He informed the fleet commander of the various incidents along the way from Tsingtao and as much as he could about the international military situation. Spee was unusually friendly and open in discussing the conflict and even philosophized briefly over the relationship between man's ignorance and the foolishness of war. The next day von Spee visited the *Cormoran* at length on a careful inspection tour. He walked the entire ship, asked pointed questions, and obviously took a concerned interest in everything along the way. After his survey von Spee concluded with a brief welcoming address to the crew, referring to their dedication and talent displayed during the trip south from Tsingtao. His conclusion suggested that the *Cormoran* was an integral part of his operational thought and could look forward to an active naval career. The crew gave a spontaneous cheer for the admiral as he left the ship. They were much impressed with his demeanor, his speech, his evident desire to use their services, and the quality of the many questions he asked during his inspection tour. The thought of possible action excited one and all.

Spee had, however, already reached a decision certain to disappoint them. Based on his discussions with Zuckschwerdt and the crew's responses to his questions, Spee thought that the *Cormoran* consumed too much coal in spite of her military prowess. She could not add sufficient firepower to his fleet to warrant her attachment. Acting with his normal promptitude, von Spee called Zuckschwerdt to a meeting that afternoon for instructions. The *Cormoran*, in conjunction with the *Prinz Eitel Friedrich*, should carry on an independent cruiser war in Australian waters. This operation would divide the Allied naval forces, mislead Allied leaders, facilitate the escape of von Spee to South American waters and, hopefully, achieve some military success. If they required additional coal, von Spee suggested that they seek out the *Emden* or *Geier*, or contact various German agencies in Batavia and Manila. In support he allotted them the collier *Mark*.

Zuckschwerdt was not particularly happy over this assignment, but von Spee disliked arguments once he had made up his mind, and the *Cormoran*'s captain posed none. The *Cormoran* moved quickly alongside the *Mark*, where the *Prinz Eitel Friedrich* was tied up on the other side. The joint mooring permitted excellent contact between the two crews. In particular, the *Cormoran*'s sailors spent every spare moment visiting their larger companion to marvel at her modern conveniences and to partake of her largess. As a former passenger liner, she had been outfitted with the best appointments possible. To destroy the elegant drapes, remove the handsome wood paneling, and create a warship had been impossible. Such action would have necessitated rebuilding the ship almost in its entirety—an attempt prohibited by the sudden onset of hostilities. Capt. Max Thierichens had begun the conversion and then gave it up as a bad job. His ship might suffer from military weakness, but she did not suffer any shortage in

luxury items. The *Prinz Eitel Friedrich* possessed a fine ice machine and an operational cold storage unit. She could, and did,
furnish frozen meat, eggs, fruit, and cool drinks with pleasant,
luxurious hospitality. The splendid tablecloths and ship's service
provided a proper setting for the expensive wines and exotic
foods.

In this active but peaceful idyll the ships' crews found a little
time to exchange a few thoughts. They conversed about the hopes
and fears inherent to war service throughout the ages and ex-
changed messages for home in the event that they did not live to
see Germany again. It was a period of high elation and emotional
hope for all. For the *Cormoran*'s crew a memorable point of their
stay was an address by an insistent Protestant pastor who demanded, and received, time to conduct a divine service at mid-
day on August 29. His message was not a highly charged paean of
patriotism but a somber approach to the perils and horrors of war.
He hoped that the men would conduct themselves with honor and
that the Fatherland might win the ultimate victory. After his
impressive sermon the pastor led the group in "Eine feste Burg
ist unser Gott." Although everyone promptly returned to work,
the words stayed with them for many months. Yet war in such
surroundings appeared as an unreal specter lost in the hazy
unknown.

Spee was contemplating the war in a more practical fashion.
With little time to consider his situation, he decided to move out
of the area somewhat ahead of his originally intended schedule.
With natural caution, he did not wish to remain in one place for
an extended time. To do so invited discovery and annihilation.
Japan's declaration of war provided the Allies with far greater
strength and flexibility in their search for the Germans. He had
to stay in front of the enemy through decisive action, good luck,
and careful planning. In the early morning of August 30 the two
cruisers with the *Titania*, *Yorck*, *Ahlers*, *Göttingen*, *Prinz Waldemar*, and *Holsatia* steamed out of Majuro. They left accompanied
by a thunderous rolling, "Hooray!" rolling from each ship they
passed on their way out of the tiny bay. Spee's squadron was off
to its fateful confrontations at Coronel and the Falkland Islands.

Even as the others departed, Zuckschwerdt decided to leave
that same day. In agreement with Thierichens he had also
changed the originally planned cruise route to the Netherlands

Indies where they hoped to undertake combat operations. There were several reasons against moving into the area off Australia. Colliers were in doubtful number, while the strong prevailing winds would soon exhaust their own limited coal supply. Beyond the fuel issue there was consideration for places to hide where coal and provisions could be transferred from a collier without too much concern for the enemy. Taking a more northern tack provided all these opportunities, and Zuckschwerdt knew from von Spee that the *Emden* and *Nürnberg* had ordered coal ships for that area. The *Mark*, exhausted of her supplies and incapable of making adequate speed, received orders to go on to the Netherlands Indies by herself, to purchase additional supplies, to recruit some Chinese sailors if possible, and to proceed with them to Limbe in the Celebes. The two raiders would meet her there for a further survey of their position and future course of action.

That afternoon the two auxiliary cruisers carefully steered their way out of the atoll and moved south to get away from the island as rapidly as possible. Just short of the equator, at a point where there was little danger of encountering enemy vessels, they made an abrupt turn westward. The following night the wireless picked up loud, clear wireless communications from at least six Japanese vessels. These sounds, continuing throughout the day of September 1, showed major enemy activities and strength in the area. Zuckschwerdt concluded that the Japanese were engaged in a wide, sweeping search for von Spee and were en route to Nauru to capture its wireless station as a secondary mission. He sought, therefore, to avoid any meeting by sailing around them. His action moved them out of range of the Japanese, but brought the *Cormoran* into hearing of Australian vessels to the south. The enemy exhibited an intense amount of activity everywhere.

Fortunately for Zuckschwerdt the radio at Nauru informed him that night that radio communication with the German station at Samoa had been interrupted for several days. The only possible conclusion was that an enemy force had occupied the island, a fact which subsequent information soon confirmed in detail. The possible hiding places had already begun to decrease in number. As they moved closer to the larger southern islands of the protectorate, both ships' wirelesses picked up repeated sounds from a German shore station. It could only be Rabaul on New Britain in the Bismarck Archipelago. They did not know about the completion of the station but its activity indicated that the government seat still remained in German hands. Zuckschwerdt decided that his circumstances demanded an effort to make contact. While the quantity of available coal there might be very small, both vessels already had to husband all their resources and take every opportunity to replenish their fast-emptying holds. To call directly upon the governor was hopelessly unrealistic. He lived with too many Australian and English settlers who would contact the enemy without delay. Zuckschwerdt knew from his earlier travels that a personal visit was not required, since there was a connecting link between Rabaul and the local governmental trading station at Kavieng on New Ireland. A small coastal steamer, the *Comet*, quartered in that area, could take a secret letter safely to Rabaul without difficulty. As a further security measure, Zuckschwerdt separated from the *Prinz Eitel Friedrich* on September 5 for the detour to the coast of New Ireland.

Timing his arrival with care, he brought the *Cormoran* smartly through the outer reefs at 7:00 A.M. the following morning. Although the German war flag hung from the proper station, the district official, Doctor Joachim Steubel, suspected a stratagem. The vessel, clearly not of recognizable German configuration, carried a well-known name on her bow, but bore little resemblance to the *Cormoran* he knew from previous visits. Steubel therefore sent his police chief to the ship, observing his progress with manifest caution through powerful field glasses. When he saw no unusual activity and a wave of invitation, Steubel cautiously approached the ship and fearfully climbed up the side. The waiting crew held their silence until his strained face peered over the railing and then joined in a general welcoming cheer. Zuckschwerdt participated in the general merriment and, as a further ensuring effort, raised the Russian flag. Should Steubel be asked subsequently about his visitor he could answer that it was a Russian merchantman.

Steubel, as luck would have it, possessed several interesting bits of information. The *Geier*, the planned replacement ship for the long-departed *Condor*, had called on him only eight days earlier. The war had caught her in the Malayan archipelago en route to her new station. She had proceeded with caution to Angaur in the Palau Islands, where she met the *Emden* and Muller had informed them about von Spee's intentions. Thereafter the *Geier* had groped her way through the unfamiliar protectorate, hoping to find a German ship. She had with her a small coal steamer whose supplies had enabled her to travel across the Pacific without difficulty. The smaller vessel had even taken the *Geier* in tow, weather conditions permitting, in order to conserve fuel. As Zuckschwerdt observed to his friend, the *Geier* and the *Cormoran* most certainly had passed very close to each other in their wanderings. Both vessels had, however, refrained from using their wireless out of respect for the many enemy cruisers plying the Pacific waters. There was no reason to attempt contact any more because they could not help one another. The *Geier* was slow and weak, and could not spare any coal. She must, like the *Cormoran*, deal with the fates of war herself.

Beyond the *Geier*'s arrival Steubel also reported that an Australian squadron, headed by the great battle cruiser of the same name, had raided Rabaul on August 12. The admiral-in-charge, Sir George Patey, had dispatched a torpedo boat into the harbor with specific instructions to destroy the radio station. The officer charged with the mission, Comdr. C. L. Cumberlege, landed with an armed party and carefully interrogated the local district officer, Ernst Tolke, who responded that there was no station in Rabaul nor were there any troops; it was a simple settlement incapable of armed resistance. Torn by a direct order from a stern admiral and an unhelpful bureaucrat, Cumberlege threatened to destroy the city by gunfire. Tolke, refusing to be intimidated, pointed out the existence of international rules against bombarding undefended cities. The officer, by that time in a savage temper, left with a few obscene phrases, wrecked the post office, tore down some telephone lines, and returned to his shop.

In the afternoon the Australian ships landed some two hundred men in the nearby area to look for the radio station as well as the absent governor, S. N. Rimburg, who had fled to the interior when war broke out. They had a good march around the countryside marred only by various minor incidents. A few soldiers entered the local mission and asked a sister about Rimburg's hiding place. She told them in short order that she was far more concerned with her school charges than with any official's location. They retired somewhat abashed. Two hours after they had come ashore, the Australians returned to their ships. One German settler complained that one of them had gained 200 marks from the former's pockets during his brief tour. They did not find the transmitter which, according to Steubel, was located in temporary quarters inland, and protected by a popular militia drawn from the local settlers. Patey had withdrawn fuming in frustration, without success.

Steubel added an explanation concerning Yap's silence. On August 12 two English cruisers, the *Minotaur* and the *Newcastle*, had moved into the island's coastal waters. They came to deprive the local population of international news and military guidance and to interrupt possible use of the wireless system for arranging coal meetings. After moving back and forth in front of the harbor, evidently fishing for the cable, the *Minotaur* had called the shore station to evacuate the building. A few minutes later the cruiser opened fire. The third shot struck the station building and destroyed it, while the eleventh shell brought down the antenna. With the mast down the *Minotaur* ceased firing, joined the *Newcastle*, and departed over the horizon. They had neglected to land a force to make certain of their success, however, which was most fortunate for the Germans. The crew of the survey vessel *Planet*, caught in the harbor by the war, had been assigned to infantry duty as defenders against any amphibious invasion. Their small vessel had been hidden in a neighboring bay and had escaped the notice of the two attackers. The *Planet's* wireless, while not a strong one, could be used for limited-range transmissions. When combined with the English failure to destroy the cable Yap-Manila-Shanghai, this simple fact provided the harried Germans with useful communication possibilities.

Zuckschwerdt welcomed these details but also asked about more immediate matters—coal supplies. Steubel responded with considerable enthusiasm that there were indeed two colliers but that no one knew their precise location. He agreed, however, to send his local ship, *Comet*, a government yacht of 977 tons, from its hiding place in a nearby inlet to Rabaul with a direct plea for the colliers' aid. The two men worked out a mutually satisfactory meeting place near Timor Island.

Everything accomplished, Zuckschwerdt saw no reason to delay a prompt departure. Steubel persuaded him to delay briefly while he provided some much-needed livestock. Zuckschwerdt readily accepted the gift, and a mixed herd of sheep and pigs soon joined the ship in a hastily constructed animal pen of dubious durability. Although the sheep proved to be poor travelers and soon wound up in the galley, the swine throve on leftovers, multiplied, and served their useful purpose through many meals. Once the animals were noisily aboard ship, the *Cormoran*'s grateful crew bade a collective farewell to their host and headed out for the open sea. Barely two hours had elapsed since their arrival.

The *Cormoran* moved back to the *Prinz Eitel Friedrich* and they set a joint course for Morotai Island at the northern entrance to the Straits of Molucca. Zuckschwerdt wanted to sail through the straits and on into the Indian Ocean. The distance to the trade routes was, however, much too great without replenishing the coal supplies. He also needed information concerning the progress of the war. After considerable discussion with Thierichens, he dispatched the latter to Limbe at the northeast corner of the Celebes to pick up information on the military situation and to order coal ships for Timor. He might also find the *Mark* there. Once the two captains had agreed on the course of action, they hastened onward, prodded by increased wireless traffic from Dutch, English, American, and Japanese transmitters in the immediate neighbourhood.

On September 11 the *Cormoran* arrived at the meeting place and hove to, since the *Prinz Eitel Friedrich* was not in sight. That evening the crew experienced one of those unusual natural phenomena often found in the tropics. As the sun descended toward darkness, its rays reflected on an unusual sea mist, and the entire ocean looked like a huge milk pail. The glittering phosphorescence created an image which reminded the more imaginative crew members of the Ice Palace in Berlin. They talked about experiences, real and imaginary, concerning that establishment and the nation's capital. The air of the equator was scarcely that of Berlin, and many a fervent prayer could be heard for just a breath of that distant fresh home atmosphere.

The following morning the ever-observant Zuckschwerdt noted that his rather leisurely cruising activity moved the ship back and forth across the equator. He immediately insisted upon inducting those crew members who had never been through the crossing-the-equator ceremonies. By noon the *Cormoran* looked more like a pleasure cruiser than a warship. The crew, bedecked in the straw hats used against the sun's heat and fabulously colored garb, played wild games to the incongruous sounds of formal march music. The band had to play the martial notes rather than the normal popular tunes because several essential players did not know anything else. It was a grand affair, far removed from the influence of the war.

As the *Prinz Eitel Friedrich* arrived that same afternoon, its crew was concerned over the revelry on the *Cormoran* heard long before seen. The party halted as soon as the luxury liner moved along side and the two crews could shout back and forth. Zuckschwerdt entertained Thierichens in his cabin, where they could discuss matters in private. The latter communicated that he had anchored near the Limbe Canal and sent a boat to the coast which had picked up a trusted German agent. The man brought with him a sheaf of war reports, but all of them came from the Reuters news agencies and recounted one German disaster after another. For Zuckschwerdt, and subsequently his crew, they presented a dismal picture at best. They finally took comfort in a small announcement that the French government had moved to Bordeaux. This action, if true, scarcely supported the other exorbitant claims. More to the point, however, were the details concerning the local situation. These were equally depressing. The Dutch had driven all coal vessels out of their territories and seized German weapons caches on Timor Island. They obviously intended to maintain an all-inclusive, strictly administered adherence to the neutrality laws. Since this neutrality obviously prevailed at their cable station, Thierichens could not possibly send off messages. He had then ordered them baked into a loaf of black bread which the German agent, hopefully, might smuggle to a friend for clandestine transmittal.

The ultimate discouragement, however, came last. Thierichen's agent had reported that the Allies had already assembled a major armada of warships and had stationed them along the entrance to the Indian Ocean. A few weeks earlier the *Emden* had passed through and the Allies had, apparently, jumped to the conclusion that other German naval elements would soon follow the same route. As meaningful was the certain Australian decision to shift trade routes over Colombo and Suez. Hunting for raiders would be difficult work and certain to require considerable time. The combination of these elements was too much for Zuckschwerdt. Without coal, without local support, without meaningful targets he could not risk even a chance encounter with real men-of-war. The situation was a good deal more difficult than he had envisaged in even his most pessimistic thoughts. But, rather than surrender entirely, he decided to search Savaii Bay on the northern coast of Ceram Island in the Dutch East Indies. Perhaps a coal steamer had reached there without discovery.

As the two vessels moved timidly deeper into the Straits of Molucca, and closer to the enemy picket line, they heard, with total clarity, his wireless messages. Fortunately for the Germans the Allies evidenced an incredible confusion of purpose. On one hand they heard an English vessel send off a credible if fake call to the *Scharnhorst* and *Gneisenau* which might well have confused even von Spee had he been listening. Quite the contrary spirit appeared in other messages, which were sent without cipher, listed names and numbers of ships, and even ordered one vessel to transmit brief notes to several other ships, all conveniently named and located for the listening Germans. There were obviously a goodly number of naval units lined up as a reception committee to meet any breakthrough attempt. Since all the identified enemy craft possessed higher speed ratings than the two raiders, the prospect for their passing through the enemy array was not a good one. To even attempt operations in an area filled with such forces would be fatally stupid. Even a rapid hit-and-run effort would cost too much coal. With the *Cormoran's* supply down to 900 tons, Zuckschwerdt could not consider lengthy, independent actions. If he did not find a collier soon, he would have to take the ship into a neutral harbor and attempt to purchase a supply. There he would likely have to choose between destruction or internment. Either one would terminate the raider's career before it really had begun. Zuckschwerdt decided, after some solitary thought, to seek a solution in Savaii Bay. Whether or not he could obtain coal there, he intended to shift his operations to a less threatening area which promised greater success at less risk.

On September 13 the lonely raiders moved into Savaii Bay. They did so with trepidation because their wireless sets hummed with innumerable Japanese messages, denoting sizable enemy activity throughout the islands. The empty bay gave temporary security, but it dashed their hopes for a collier. Romantic souls found some compensation in the unbelievable magnificence of the natural scenery. The water was a green glass mirror without a disfiguring ripple. It melded into the splendid multishaded green foliage decorated with a rainbow of flowers, through which moved equally colorful cockatoos and horn-billed parrots. This spectacular sight rolled up the slopes of several high mountains surrounding the bay. For a moment the Germans forgot the threat of destruction and set aside the constant strain imposed by nature and human foe. Before they could indulge in too many fantasies a small cutter, moving out from the jungle shore, destroyed the image of nature in the raw. At her stern the Dutch flag stood out in flat relief. One of the occupants had on a uniform, reflecting an official status as well as providing an instant explanation for the lack of a ship in the empty bay.

Zuckschwerdt, hoping to obtain some information on local events as well as more military news from the world at large, decided to talk with the man. The elegantly attired Dutchman, his face stained black by the sun, with a finely formed beard, greeted his visitor politely, but declined the invitation to come aboard or even to discuss the war. He pointedly did not bother to ask questions in return. After the uncommunicative exchange, the official boat put about and circled the *Cormoran*, while the bureaucrat made careful notes in a large notebook. Obviously satisfied, he had the helmsman turn toward the *Prinz Eitel Friedrich*. Thierichens, however, did not wish to reveal the name or details of his vessel and turned away. The Dutchman, in his tiny boat, was persistent and tried to get around by increasing his speed. Because of an apparent reef, the angle of original encounter, and Thierichens's determination, the cutter could not get around its prey. After something more than two turns on this curious carousel, the two vessels, a David and Goliath, remained bow to bow. After a worried pause the Dutchman quickly sketched something in his pad, using his thumb as an artist's measure, and then pushed his tiny command out to sea where he had at least a full day's run to the next wireless station.

The strange circumstances of the entire affair prompted the *Cormoran*'s crew to look over the stern of their vessel to see what the observer had copied. To their chagrin they discovered that they had indeed erased *Rjasan* but had not removed Vladivostok! Since *Cormoran* had not been painted on either, the Dutchman had some grounds for confusion over the apparent Russian ship with the German crew.

The unfriendly official's determined attitude renewed Zuck-schwerdt's respect for the Dutch approach to neutrality. There was no doubt now that the Germans would not find any support in the tiny protectorate. Unfortunately he had no way to ascertain where the colliers might have found new locations to await their countrymen, although he assumed that they might move northward on the high seas to positions near the southern Philippine Islands. To gain contact with them he would need to break wireless silence, an action certain to draw the enemy's attention. As a security measure Zuckschwerdt ordered the two vessels back out to sea, where he could undertake transmissions while setting a false course.

They soon entered the reef-filled waters between the island of Halmahera and the coast of New Guinea. That night both vessels alternated in filling the air with full-power wireless messages directed toward all points of the compass. They called every possible steamer, with a concentrated effort to reach the *Mark*. There was no response. Unknown to Zuckschwerdt, the *Mark* was doing her best, but could not escape the unwanted attentions of English auxiliary cruisers, who drove her into hiding. More disturbing in the darkness to the two raiders was the crackle of communications between Japanese torpedo boats. All hands were certain that the fruitless search for coal had pinpointed their location for the enemy locusts who would appear at dawn. When the sun broke through the darkness on September 14, both crews were at action stations, ready to meet the anticipated enemy onslaught. For two hours the anxious eyes of every crew member searched for the first signs of enemy vessels. Despite their concern, none appeared. By noon they were back in open water, far from land, and certain no one had detected their presence.

The new direction denoted a total shift in the aspirations for both the *Cormoran* and the *Prinz Eitel Friedrich*. They had escaped the prison of Tsingtao, met von Spee in the Marshalls, and returned for offensive operations. Their hopes had for these operations to be buried for lack of fuel, *Emden*'s growing success in other battles, and the lack of adequate knowledge concerning the war's progress elsewhere. They were now forced to strike out on their own and shift for themselves. Without answer to the wireless calls, but with continuously diminishing coal supplies, they were in serious trouble.

Chapter 4 Action

Zuckschwerdt invited Thierichens aboard the *Cormoran* during the afternoon of September 14. In serious discourse about the uncertain future, they agreed to a number of fundamental points. Remembering their earlier visit to Kavieng they decided that Yap held several advantages for their mutual purposes. If the cable station was still able to function, the officials could provide the latest intelligence on the conflict, as well as a complete situation report on the current possibilities for obtaining coal. At the same time they talked about visiting Angaur in the Palau Islands, where Muller had found coal for the *Emden*'s trip into the Indian Ocean. In addition to the chance possibility of finding precious fuel in that area, there was reason to hope that the message left on Kavieng might have had some effect. If the Rabaul authorities had sent off the *Comet* or another vessel to the Palaus, it would be just arriving at that destination. In either Angaur or Yap, however, there was no certainty that the Japanese had not already occupied the islands. They had, during previous years, indicated unusual concern in the eventual fate of both of them. The two captains agreed that, under such circumstances, they should not endanger both ships by entering either harbor together. Some type of divided effort or a probe by one of them was in order.

Thierichens went on, however, to point out that the *Prinz Eitel Friedrich*'s length would not permit her to enter the reef-enclosed facilities at Yap, and, thereby, simplified the final decision. Zuckschwerdt agreed immediately that Thierichens should strike out for Angaur and, if unsuccessful in locating a collier, cruise the other nearby islands. If this search failed, then he would proceed to Sturm Island. The *Cormoran* would go to Yap, take on coal if possible, and send telegrams to Manila and Batavia asking for coal deliveries to that location. Thereafter he would take a circuitous route to the rendezvous point at Sturm Island. In the event of the slightest indication of difficulty, they agreed upon a special distress signal. Otherwise they proposed strict radio silence to avoid alerting listening Allied vessels that the Germans were back in the area. They shook hands, wished each other good fortune, and parted for their respective missions.

As Thierichens clambered back on the *Prinz Eitel Friedrich*, he noted an unusual stir and demanded some explanation. His subordinate officers quickly took him aside and informed him that, during his brief absence, the wireless operator had committed the flagrant error of dispatching an unciphered message to the *Mark*. The very angry captain had to return to the *Cormoran* in haste to tell Zuckschwerdt about the security error. Confronted with this possible exposure of his plans, the latter ordered an immediate shift of their eventual destination from Sturm Island to Alexis Harbor in Kaiser Wilhelm's Land. He was satisfied that it was in many ways a better choice in terms of location and accessibility, as well as a place well known to the old *Cormoran* crew. Hidden in a deeply cut bay surrounded by impenetrable forests, the harbor provided a fine haven free from external observation and surprise. Thierichens returned to his command a second time in a savage humor, a sharp contrast to Zuckschwerdt who was, for this time, more philosophical about the error than he might have been under other circumstances.

Although the decision to part was clear, the two vessels had some distance to travel in the same direction. They chose to do so in a close tandem position, irrespective of proper wartime naval measures. The weather was too clear, the sea too calm, the camaraderie too great to avoid a final exchange between the ship's crews. They rigged up a line from one to the other and passed various personal mementos back and forth, as well as a carefully lined basket which ferried cold beer to the *Cormoran*. The cold drinks served both to slake the men's thirst and to remind them that they must now return to the war with all its rigors. All the luxuries from the *Prinz Eitel Friedrich* would soon be matters of envious reminiscence. Shortly after noon on September 15 they separated once more and moved off into the unknown. They were not to meet again.

The next night, that of September 16, Zuckschwerdt spent in

the wireless cabin, impatiently disturbing the operators with his nervous footsteps in their confined space. He knew that the *Prinz Eitel Friedrich* should have arrived in Angaur and needed to learn if there had been an unfriendly reception committee. When no sound came from the wireless, he slowly relaxed and, shortly before midnight, told one of his staff officers that all would go well in Yap as well. The following morning the observers high in the ship's rigging saw the bare, stark outline of Yap, but they could not see any ship in the harbor. Zuckschwerdt ordered one of his floodlights turned on as a signal to the German officials that a German vessel was coming into the harbor. The crew of the *Planet*, which was in the harbor, recognized the signal and responded with a counter light partially blanked out to make a star design. It proved that the feared Japanese force was not present. Unfortunately not everyone understood these unrehearsed signals, and some of the local women thought that the ship's flashing light was really gun flashes. They remembered all too well the bright light, followed by the ear-splitting roar of shells and resultant destruction, occasioned by the earlier English visit. They immediately packed a few valuables and fled to the inner recesses of the island. When they discovered their understandable error, they returned to the harbor for the *Cormoran*'s arrival.

Zuckschwerdt brought his vessel through the outer coral mounds with exemplary speed and skill. Although he had visited the cable station many times, he had a different vessel to navigate, without the normal harbor guiding buoys and landmarks as guideposts.

With effortless ease he moved to the inner pier, and the eager landing party climbed down to tie the lines securely to the aged bollards. Right behind them came the entire crew, boisterously pushing and shoving their way down a single precarious gangplank. While it buckled and swayed in a fashion certain to bring alarm to timorous souls, few held back from the hurried rush for terra firma. Yap was the first land they had stepped on since leaving Tsingtao. Immediately the human wave broke up to enclose islands of old friends and moved on to the Coconut, a tavern of insular fame and charm, to celebrate the unexpected convocation. The reunions were notable to say the least.

Although he encouraged his men to take advantage of the local facilities, Zuckschwerdt busied himself with more pressing concerns. The *Planet*'s captain, Oswald Collmann, hurried on board the *Cormoran* with the latest telegrams and reports. He knew the raider's major concern without being asked. Even before he read the reports, however, Zuckschwerdt handed Collman a sheaf of messages for dispatch—all fervent pleas for coal. Collmann complied, and Yap's limited wireless facilities soon throbbed with the effort to meet the challenge. Moreover, as the answers to Zuckschwerdt's messages asking for coal trickled back, and not all of them did so, they brought only unpleasant news. There was no fuel to be had anyplace. The German colliers were on the run and, for the most part, had either been captured or driven into neutral harbors guarded by enemy ships. There could be no help.

Once these transactions were in motion, Zuckschwerdt relaxed a bit and asked Collmann about the *Planet* and Yap. The latter reported that he had brought his ship into the harbor on August 7 and had begun immediate defense preparations. Although he had used every available man and weapon, Collmann realized that a serious defense was out of the question. His preparations had barely begun when, on August 12, the English cruisers *Minotaur* and *Newcastle* had unexpectedly appeared and had conducted their destructive bombardment. The resourceful Collmann had promptly salvaged the pieces of the destroyed installations and combined them with the supplies on the *Planet*. Within two days he had a functioning reserve station with a range of 300 sea miles.

Since the raid no further enemy ships had been seen in the vicinity, although their wireless traffic was a constant reminder of their omnipresent authority. Subsequently the German steamship, *Princess Alice*, and the chartered American collier, *Rio Passiq*, had stopped for a brief visit en route to the Palaus. No one on Yap could guess their fate, but they had not left any coal for following vessels.

A desperate Zuckschwerdt, however, did manage to persuade his host to part with 165 tons of coal. While it was not nearly enough to inspire confidence, it did raise the *Cormoran*'s total supply to 850 tons. Once he had the coal loaded, Zuckschwerdt found no reason to remain at Yap and issued orders for an early departure. He accelerated these preparations when the wireless picked up an anonymous report that the Australians had occupied German New Guinea. If true the *Prinz Eitel Friedrich* was in considerable danger because Thierichens would not have the news before his departure from Angaur. When he arrived in Alexis Harbor he might find a most unpleasant surprise. In order to warn his friend Zuckschwerdt had the lines cast off at noon on September 19, and the *Cormoran*, bearing a sorrowful crew, pushed back out to sea. Their land visit, after a month at sea, had been short. Throughout the afternoon and evening the *Cormoran* wireless operators sought to contact the *Prinz Eitel Friedrich*, using their disaster signal, but received no response. Without an answer Zuckschwerdt decided to visit Alexis Harbor himself.

The trip was uneventful, and in the early morning mists of September 23 the *Cormoran* pushed into the harbor. With everyone at action stations and ready to fight, Zuckschwerdt dropped anchor in the outer harbor near St. Michael's Catholic Mission. The senior priest came immediately on board and reported that no enemy vessel had been there; the earlier report was entirely false. On the other hand the *Prinz Eitel Friedrich* had not arrived nor, more serious in immediate portent, had the two colliers from Rabaul. The latter were twelve days overdue. Zuckschwerdt, most concerned about this new development, walked slowly around the *Cormoran* while contemplating his situation in some detail. Under all the circumstances he had few alternatives to staying in the harbor until he learned more about both the *Prinz Eitel Friedrich* and the colliers. Although they were unlikely to arrive after the set time lapse, he had no other choices. By the time he had made the second round of the ship, Zuckschwerdt had accepted his obvious position and was more involved with surveying the harbor.

He knew the anchorage from earlier trips but had not observed the area with a war in mind. It was located on a relatively straight coastline seven miles north of the government seat at Friedrich Wilhelm's Harbor. Although one could see the other settlement, transportation between them was less simple. Small reef islands, reaching one or two meters above the water, partially covered with high jungle trees and dense foliage, were scattered along the shore. Passing between these soil mounds and the mainland was, because of many perpendicular, jagged reefs, possible only for adventuresome small boats. Alexis Harbor, was then, a fine anchorage, well-removed from the probable focal point of any enemy action. Zuckschwerdt also remembered that far back in the harbor was Bostrem Bay. This improper designation belonged to a narrow, winding defile overgrown by the jungle vegetation. It was a superlative hiding place, almost impenetrable, and known only to the local inhabitants. Under these circumstances Zuckschwerdt moved the *Cormoran* back toward the edge of Bostrem Bay but not into it. The inner area was the private domain of vast numbers of ferocious mosquitos.

As a further precautionary measure Zuckschwerdt wanted a lookout post erected on one of the small outer islands, Sek. He noted a huge tree whose crown dominated the entire surrounding jungle. It was ideally situated for observing all activities along the coast for many miles. He ordered the crew to build a rudimentary lookout station in the tree. His instructions were clear and simple but neglected the details concerning their implementation. The crew members assigned to the chore had very little idea about how to implement their orders. Fortunately they had one of the New Guineans recruited in Tsingtao with them. Without a word he grabbed a vine hanging down from the tree and, gripping it between his fingers and toes, inched his way up the thin jungle rope to a higher point where other plants clinging to the tree offered better travel possibilities. At a height of some twenty meters he found a stout limb. Using a strong rope drawn up from the ground he pulled a large plank up and fastened it to his perch.

This tenuous platform became the main support for the observers, who took turns climbing up to the treetop, perhaps fifteen meters higher. The sailors rapidly stocked their halfway station with supplies and two sets of signal flags. Before long they were taking turns climbing up and down like errant schoolboys. The climb created a curious ambivalence among the participants, exhilarated by the beautiful scenery even as they suffered the fatigue of a strenuous climb under a hot tropical sun. Although crude in both appearance and function, the tree perch could serve the *Cormoran* as an early warning system and give Zuckschwerdt time to decide whether to fight, run, or hide.

In an effort to supplement any visual information, Zuckschwerdt sent the local missionary boat to Friedrich Wilhelm's Harbor to bring the district officer back for a discussion about local events. The three men assigned the task simply rowed to the neighboring village and walked up to the only distinctive building. Their man, Dr. Karl Gebhard, was more than a little nonplussed by their arrival but readily agreed to accompany them back to the ship. They did, as a security measure, return to the boat by a more circuitous route and rowed back without alerting anyone. To Zuckschwerdt's intense disappointment, Gebhard could tell him nothing. The war was a long way from Kaiser Wilhelm's Land. Gebhard agreed to direct any colliers which might wander into Kaiser Wilhelm's Harbor toward the *Cormoran*, but he could do no more.

Without real news the *Cormoran*'s crew spent the next day preparing for a longer stay. That night, however, the wireless operators reported to Zuckschwerdt that they could hear the Australian battle cruiser *Australia* loud and clear. She must be close. Zuckschwerdt listened to the reports himself and, as they became more distinct, grew far more apprehensive concerning the following day. His fears were well-founded.

The next morning, just after seven o'clock, four large ships materialized out of the early morning fog surrounding the swampy coast. In order not to miss the harbor, which was always difficult to find, they had moved much closer to the shoreline than was navigationally safe and had escaped detection until the last possible moment. From an immediate study of their lines the observers decided that they were the *Australia*, the Australian cruiser *Encounter*, the French armored cruiser *Montcalm*, and the armed transport cruiser *Berrima*, of 11,120 tons. The *Encounter* and the *Berrima* moved slowly into Alexis Harbor. For the *Cormoran*'s crew the immediate sight of major enemy naval units provided an adrenal shock. Action, of course, was unthinkable. One salvo from any of the three cruisers would blow the *Cormoran* into uncountable pieces. Nonetheless Zuckschwerdt issued, for the first time, the serious order, "Clear for action!" and added, as everyone watched the Australians with scarcely a breath, instructions to weigh anchor and start the ship's engines.

By this time the *Encounter* was some 100 meters away. The *Cormoran*'s sailors steeled themselves for the first shell's impact. They were convinced that the natural overhang and miniscule intervening pieces of coral could never protect protect them from discovery. Nonetheless Zuckschwerdt, with the engine humming, ordered the ship turned around in order to move her into the nearby Bostrem Bay. Ever so slowly the *Cormoran* moved around, at one time exposing her broad side to the *Encounter*. The frightened Germans were sure that this maneuver had to alert the Australians, individually clearly discernible and audible only a stone's throw away. With the majestic calm more possible for ships than humans, the *Cormoran* gracefully retired into the previously selected hiding place. No one paid the slightest heed to the mosquitoes, who attacked this invasion in force. The ship, a bit too sluggish for the frightened crew, disappeared into the dense overgrowth.

Once past the first bend, Zuckschwerdt ordered the ship anchored at the best possible angle to block the waterway and to bring all possible guns to bear on the entryway. With two quick adjustments he succeeded in giving a good field of fire to four guns. Concurrently he dispatched two landing guns and four machine guns to the bend of the bay and a makeshift series of rifle units into the bush. Without real training or soldierly understanding the sailor infantrymen pushed blindly ashore and frantically established a makeshift defensive line. Within a short time they were ready to meet the enemy. Zuckschwerdt was now much more confident of his position, because he could give the following Australians a good blow or two in the confined area. They might be able to bring indirect fire on the Germans over the intervening landmass but their accuracy would be dubious at best.

He then found that good fortune remained with him. The ship's lookout, who could see the tree observation post, soon made visual contact. Using the semaphore system, the tree group kept Zuckschwerdt well informed of the enemy's activities. An incongruous note in the serious work of one observation post was the wild gyrations of a white cockatoo family which chose that time to return to its home. Finding it occupied by an unknown band of animals, they flew around the tree screaming their displeasure. The desperate sailors in the tree were pleased now to have a dual set of signal flags. While one set served to keep the ship informed, the other provided the means of defense against the disgruntled birds.

Within a short time the makeshift communications system reported that the two ships were leaving the harbor. Zuckschwerdt refused to believe the message. When it was repeated, he insisted that it must be a *ruse de guerre*. No warship, for the first time in an enemy area, could be so careless. There had to be another explanation and he kept his forces in a steady alert position. Shortly afterward the *Cormoran*'s wireless operator hurried to the captain and reported that the admiral on board the *Australia* had given a signal in plain English to make steam for a speed of sixteen knots. Quite obviously they had not noted the raider nor its movements. Zuckschwerdt promptly informed his crew, who collapsed from the effects of the strain. Some cried, others cheered, others simply remained speechless. Many now found time to attack the mosquitoes, whose unobstructed success had already given some men the appearance of having a bad case of hives.

Zuckschwerdt, now watching his observation post through his own glasses, learned that the two heavier cruisers were moving back and forth in a large circle outside Friedrich Wilhelm's Harbor, firing a few random shots, probably to impress the natives. The two remaining ships had dropped anchor in the harbor. Because of their location, which blocked the line of sight, they effectively screened off the German observers. Zuckschwerdt concluded that the Australians must be putting troops ashore.

At five o'clock the Australian squadron lifted anchor and departed. Shortly thereafter Dr. Gebhard returned to the *Cormoran* with a report of the day's events. He had watched everything from a little hill behind the German settlement. The Australians had landed a force that he estimated to be 100 men with their equipment. Apparently they intended to stay for a while. Zuckschwerdt immediately decided to attack the landing party. He saw an opportunity to damage the enemy while bringing some glory to his ship. Gebhard, who knew the area, enthusiastically agreed to the proposal and, together with Zuckschwerdt, worked out a simple plan. The settlement in Friedrich Wilhelm's Harbor was located on a small peninsula and could be cut off from the mainland.

If the Germans could move at night, with the official as guide, to positions behind the village, they might attack out of the jungle immediately after sunrise. The *Cormoran*, taking the example of that morning, would use the early haze as concealment to approach the harbor, and then, concurrent with the land assault, blanket the Australian camp with shellfire. Under these circumstances there was only a single shortcoming worth serious consideration. The Germans had to be certain that the enemy ships would not return to the area. If they did reappear, the *Cormoran*, and the operation, would not last many minutes. More intelligence was necessary, and Gebhard agreed to return to the occupied town for additional details. Promising a speedy report back to the ship, he left on his assignment.

That night, more than a little fatigued, Gebhard returned to the *Cormoran*. It was 1:30 in the morning, and he had to wake Zuckschwerdt from a sound sleep. With him came a friend from the settlement who had been there throughout the Australian landing. They brought with them a letter from the Australian commander to Gebhard, little more than a copy of an earlier declaration by the acting German governor of New Guinea, E. Haber.

On September 11 Admiral Patey had sent a crudely translated note to Haber in New Britain, pointing out the total futility of resistance. Haber replied that he could not hand over the protectorate to the Australians; only the German emperor could do that. On the other hand, he agreed that he obviously could not prevent the occupation and advised all the local officials scattered throughout the area not to resist the Australians. To this statement Patey appended his personal injunction, underscoring his armed strength, determination, and desire for a prompt response. He also set forth an official statement that his country was replacing the German administration with its own. If the local settlers would give a written declaration of neutrality, they could remain without fear of disturbance. This paper was of little purport to Zuckschwerdt, beyond establishing the permanence of Australian interest. Gebhard added, however, that the Australians had actually landed 250 men and intended to return the following morning in full force. This news snapped the sleepy captain to rigid attention. He had to leave immediately.

Once again the sole possible decision posed a serious problem. To leave a little-known, forested area in the middle of the night required an undue amount of self-confidence and good luck. There was, unhappily, no alternative beyond destruction, and Zuckschwerdt ordered a prompt departure. Employing men with the smallest available lights along both the port and starboard sides of the ship, he maneuvered the *Cormoran* out of Bostrem Bay. By three o'clock they reached the reef exit of Alexis Harbor, where Zuckschwerdt paused for a brief moment of thought. He had to be away from the coast before first light—a time limit just over two hours away.

His memory served him well in making a decision on which

By the eve of World War I in July 1914, Adalbert Zuckschwerdt, captain of the *Cormoran*, had served nearly four
years in the Far East. Handsome, popular, he was known to
virtually everyone in the various navies in the Orient. By
1943, as depicted here, he was a rear admiral.—Photograph
courtesy of H. Hildebrand

The original *Cormoran* in Tsingtao, 1914. Built in 1892, a cruiser of 1,630 tons, with a speed in excess of fifteen knots, and mounting eight 4.1-inch guns, *Cormoran* was by 1914 obsolescent and demoted to the less glamorous, if more proper, designation of gunboat.—Photograph courtesy of Fritz Bayer

Upon disablement of the original *Cormoran* on August 5, 1914, Captain Zuckschwerdt oversaw the rapid conversion of the captured Russian steamer *Rjasan* into a commerce raider, with the name *Cormoran* to confuse the enemy. Displacing some 5,100 tons, she could make fourteen knots, and was armed with eight 4-inch guns—some of which are clearly visible in this photograph taken in internment in Apra Harbor, Guam, in 1916.—Photograph courtesy of Carmelita Ortiz

Crewmen of the *Cormoran* in Lamotrek Island, in the West Carolines, about 380 miles south of Guam. Here the raider hid from overwhelming enemy naval forces from October 12 to December 12, 1914, while a cutter was dispatched to Guam seeking sources of provisions and coal.
—Photograph courtesy of Marineschule Muerwik

While in Lamotrek, the crew of the *Cormoran* maintained an active social life with the natives, engaging in boat races, swimming contests, and costume parties. Upon the ship's departure for Guam on December 12 at least three known romances ended with tearful good-byes. Here native girls perform a farewell dance.—Photograph courtesy of Marineschule Muerwik

Preparing the lines to coal the *Cormoran*, Apra Harbor, Guam. While interned in Guam from December 14, 1914, to April 7, 1917, the ship was allowed to keep enough coal on board to enable it to steam to the open sea should a storm threaten the not overly well protected harbor. —Photograph courtesy of Fritz Bayer

A happy outing of the *Cormoran*'s crew in 1916. During the interment in Guam, after the governorship of the island changed and the ship was totally disarmed in early 1916, the Germans were treated as friendly guests and allowed to enjoy the social life of the island.—Photograph courtesy of Carmelita Ortiz

By the time the Germans arrived in Guam in December 1914, they had among
the crew twenty-nine South Sea Islanders, some of whom are shown on board the
Cormoran during its voyage.—Photograph courtesy of Adolf Niezechowski-Voss

Some of the South Sea Islanders of the *Cormoran* performing an exhibition of
spear throwing at a Guam fair in July 1918.—Photograph courtesy of Marineschule Muerwik

The U.S.S. *Supply*, which made quarterly trips transporting goods for Guam, in Apra Harbor, 1914–17. After the *Cormoran* was scuttled on April 7, 1917, this vessel participated in the rescue of the German crew.—Photograph courtesy of United States National Archives

During the scuttling of the *Cormoran*, seven of the crew lost their lives. The searching Americans recovered six bodies, which were buried with full military honors. A simple cement monument, erected by the Germans in 1917, was placed over the graves with the inscription, "They gave their lives for the honor of the flag."—Photograph courtesy of Marineschule Muerwik

direction he must take for escape. He remembered from a social outing during an earlier visit that some twenty miles north of the harbor was a volcanic island called Dampier. It was surrounded by treacherous reefs and was considered far too dangerous for normal shipping traffic. Even the most adventuresome sailor avoided its navigational hazards. At the same time Zuckschwerdt realized that the strong current running in that direction would accelerate the *Cormoran*'s speed. A final clinching point was the local natives' habit of lighting huge fires to observe and celebrate the passing ships. Since time schedules were never precise the fires were not overly helpful in providing information about ships' movements. If the *Cormoran* moved at full speed, she would heat up sufficiently to throw flames over the mouths of her low funnels. These telltale red lights of intense human activity aboard ship needed the camouflage support of the kanaka fires. The hesitation, in the face of the immediate Australian threat, lasted only a few moments, and Zuckschwerdt ordered full speed ahead for Dampier. As soon as he issued the directive, he uttered a few audible fervent phrases soliciting divine indulgence.

As his instructions obtained a prompt response from the ship's engine room, the *Cormoran* soon rocked and twisted under the strain. Nonetheless the sailors soon felt the prompt impact of the fast-moving current which accelerated the *Cormoran*'s speed to record rates. At just the right moment fires appeared along the shore to both confuse any wakeful Australian and to help light the way northward. Twice the ominous scrape of metal over coral threatened both the ship's safety and the crew's morale, but there was no halt. By dawn the *Cormoran* was once more free and running. Gebhard who had now joined the ship's company as a reserve officer was highly impressed with the captain's daring and determination.

Zuckschwerdt promptly thought about his friend Thierichens and tried again to establish wireless contact with the *Prinz Eitel Friedrich*. At least nine days should have passed since the former luxury liner had reached Angaur, and she should be moving back on Alexis Harbor for the promised meeting with the *Cormoran*. All day, using the highest possible power intensity, the *Cormoran*'s wireless sent out intermittent alarm signals without response. That night they had to be halted because the Australian communication sounds were much too close for safety. Without knowing what had happened to his friend, Zuckschwerdt opted to turn back to Yap in search of general information and the *Prinz Eitel Friedrich*. The return trip was an easy affair, with excellent weather and no visible sign of enemy activity. As the ship approached Yap for the second time, during the afternoon of September 28, Zuckschwerdt sent out a cautious low-powered wireless call to find out if the island remained in German control. The reserve station built up by the *Planet*'s crew responded almost immediately that the *Cormoran* could enter the harbor without concern. No enemy had bothered them since the long-past destructive cruiser attack. Shortly after 4:00 P.M. the crew was once more ashore to meet old friends and argue about the seating at the Coconut.

In general the news of events elsewhere was far more cheering than it had been during their earlier visit. They learned about the great successes of the *U-9* in sinking three English cruisers, of the *Emden*'s growing list of victories, and of the cruiser squadron's cutting of the Canadian-Australian cable lines. Even more immediately pleasant was the news that a coal steamer was en route to save them.

That evening the conscientious Zuckschwerdt had the wireless operator seek contact with the *Prinz Eitel Friedrich*. He promptly had a response. Thierichens had managed to pick up 3,000 tons of coal in the Palau Islands and had departed Angaur just ahead of the Australian cruiser *Sydney*. He had slipped into Alexis Harbor and had learned there of the *Cormoran*'s close escape. At the same time he had escaped observation from the unwary Australians and departed without alerting the enemy. In view of all these developments, he had decided to drop all operational aspirations and had ordered the *Prinz Eitel Friedrich* to South America. Zuckschwerdt, called away from a local party in his honor, rushed back to the ship and tried to raise the *Prinz Eitel Friedrich* again for direct discussions, but the atmospheric conditions caused too much static. The *Cormoran* was alone. To complete this depressing feeling, a message arrived a few hours later stating that the steamer scheduled for her aid had encountered an English warship and had been forced back into Manila. There were no other available colliers.

Dispirited, Zuckschwerdt spent all of September 28 sending

out messages, seeking a responsive friend. His coal supply was down to 495 tons, which precluded serious activity or distant movement. If the *Prinz Eitel Friedrich* could be found she might return and divide her coal, and then the two vessels could combine their strengths and attack enemy positions for additional fuel. His efforts found only silence. Then, without warning, the wireless of the *Australia* rudely interrupted these transmissions. Whether she was simply irritated at the German efforts or actively seeking to block contact remained uncertain, but she was obviously in the vicinity. The *Cormoran's* personnel estimated that she was less than 200 miles from Yap and moving in their direction. There could be no more effort to contact anyone. On the contrary the great cruiser should probably arrive the following afternoon.

Her presence indicated to Zuckschwerdt that the Australians had occupied the southern islands and had now begun their move northward to occupy territory and search out surviving German shipping. At the same time he realized that the great size of the protectorates and limited enemy resources precluded a consistent pattern of surveillance. While occasional patrols assured some control, there would, of necessity, be many blank spots in the control system. Under the immediate stress for fuel and a possible confrontation with the *Australia*, Zuckschwerdt renewed his determination to catch the Australian landing force at Friedrich Wilhelm's Harbor. There were, however, an estimated 250 men in that party, which far outnumbered the 100 men he could muster for the operation. The indomitable Zuckschwerdt decided to talk to the *Planet's* crew.

In a hastily assembled meeting with that ship's officers he reflected, for their benefit, upon the movement of von Spee's cruiser squadron to South America, the continued decline in Yap's military significance, the impossibility of mounting an effective defense against the *Australia*, and the need for a German success someplace in the protectorate. After this lengthy discourse he proposed that the *Planet's* crew join the *Cormoran* as naval infantry for a joint assault against the Australians. A victory would do wonders for German morale throughout the world. Further maintenance of Yap was valueless and the *Planet's* sailors would be more useful supporting the *Cormoran's* effectiveness rather than falling into enemy hands after a brief face-saving resistance. It was not impossible that *Cormoran* might find another ship suitable for conversion to an auxiliary cruiser. There was no opposition, not even a question; his case was obvious. Nevertheless, Zuckschwerdt gave them no time to reflect. He had the *Planet*'s crew dismantle their defensive weapons and carry them on board the *Cormoran*, in addition to loading the last 40 tons of coal still on the island. The new recruits brought with them all the ammunition and foodstuffs that they could store on board. As they crowded up the gangplank, Zuckschwerdt suddenly realized that he did not have an adequate supply of landing boats for the proposed operation. He decided to bring along a small traffic vessel, the *Lloyd*, of something less than 150 tons displacement. In order to conserve fuel they would tow her as far as they could. As for the *Planet*, he made hurried preparations to blow her up and left a few men on the island for that purpose. He also ordered them to systematically destroy all military equipment. When the Allies did reach the island, they should find only the natives.

On September 30 the *Cormoran* put back out to sea. The final farewells brought mixed emotions. For the inhabitants of the island they had the release from military concern. As an undefended place, Yap would not be a battleground when the enemy did arrive to begin his occupation. While they were relieved and cheered by this prospect, they were saddened at the realization that the German flag would soon come down for the final time. Old friends would not be seen again. For the *Cormoran*, the departure was not a pleasant augury. The *Cormoran*'s last friendly landing point was gone, and the beer at the Coconut would become only a pleasant dream. *Cormoran* would have to conquer its next port of call. The added manpower provided a better military force but also cramped the normal living habits of the crew. With such a large complement, every human problem whether over food, duties, or sports, was instantly magnified many times. Nonetheless Zuckschwerdt took the risk that action or the possibility thereof would keep the men in check. Setting a fake course due north until he lost sight of Yap, he then turned around for Friedrich Wilhelm's Harbor. There was no need to give the enemy any warning.

As he moved back on the well-traveled path southward, Zuckschwerdt renewed his efforts to reach the *Prinz Eitel Friedrich*.

In the early evening of October 1 the wireless crew made contact with Thierichens, 1,150 miles away. A frantically happy Zuckschwerdt ran to the wireless room and sent off a plea for joint action. But in the middle of it the *Australia*, for reasons known only to her commander, increased her sound intensity and blocked further exchange. There would be no more discussion. While Zuckschwerdt fumed over this unwanted development the sea suddenly grew much rougher and there was more serious work closer at hand. High waves soon cascaded over the ship in increasing force, breaking the lines connecting the *Cormoran* with the *Lloyd*. Valuable time and human energy were lost in the struggle to recover them. In this battle with the elements, the press of foul weather, extra naval duties, and the presence of the *Planet*'s crew brought many problems. Despite the best of intentions, the crew remained constantly under foot and finally huddled together like lost mice in various odd corners. The crewmen could not train for their amphibious action, and their overcrowded conditions made life generally miserable.

The weather remained bad throughout the trip. On October 5 the *Cormoran* began her approach on Friedrich Wilhelm's Harbor. That night, while still some seventy miles away, Zuckschwerdt decided to stop and listen for the enemy's wireless exchanges. It had scarcely grown dark when the tempo of this traffic reached major proportions. At least three warships were close by, including the French *Montcalm*. They must be in the harbor or very close to the coast. Any attempt to mount an attack would surely bring them into action, and the outcome would obviously be fatal to the single aggressor. Zuckschwerdt, with great reluctance, decided to move back on Yap. If the Germans still held the island, he might use the cable again in a final plea for coal.

En route back to Yap the ship's course passed close to Maron Island in the Hermit Islands. Much earlier the South Sea firm of H. R. Wahlen, with its central office there, had been most helpful to the *Planet* during a survey call. Hoping to find a few tons of coal, Zuckschwerdt decided to stop. During the night of October 6 the *Cormoran* arrived and, knowing the reefs through the *Planet*'s captain, entered the main lagoon by moonlight. The inhabitants assumed that the strange vessel must be friendly, because no other ship had dared attempt the passage at night. Representatives of the company approached her with some care, however, and did not draw near the ship until she finally dropped her anchor at one o'clock. Fortunately Captain Collmann recognized one of the men and called him by his nickname, "Benzin." Thereafter the *Cormoran*'s crew quickly accepted the friendly hospitality displayed by the island representatives despite the unseemly hour. Nonetheless there was no coal, and the *Cormoran* departed the following day. Zuckschwerdt left the *Lloyd* to the company as a present. She was no longer useful and had caused sufficient difficulties already.

As he reapproached Yap, Zuckschwerdt had to be extra cautious. He no longer could determine whether it was still in German hands or not. By listening to wireless traffic, his sole intelligence tool, he realized that eight Japanese ships were around him, including some major units. He could not attempt even a cautious call to the island's reserve station, for the enemy would then pinpoint the *Cormoran* immediately and cut her off in the harbor within a few hours. There was no alternative to taking the ship in without previous announcement. He carefully worked out the vagaries of speed, distance, and probable weather to bring the *Cormoran* into Yap shortly before sunset on October 8. Darkness in the tropics comes with the sudden finality and totality of a theatre curtain. There is little dusk, little quietude of evening. Day and night have a definite, common frontier. If something were amiss, Zuckschwerdt might be able to run fast enough to escape into the night's enveloping blackness.

The late afternoon was very stormy, with high winds and heavy rains. Dark clouds obscured vision, while the intermittent squalls kept the sailors soaked to the skin. In such weather Yap was normally covered by a heavy mattress of clouds, which made navigation a most challenging affair. One was dangerously close to land before one suddenly saw the island's outline before him. As the *Cormoran* emerged from the dark, misty haze of a storm cloud between 7 and 8 o'clock, virtually everyone forward observed the harbor entrance directly before them. At the same time they saw, perhaps 150 meters from them, the overwhelming shape of a Japanese battleship, the *Satsuma*. Her 19,000 tons and jutting armament of four 12-inch and eight 10-inch guns provided an awesome display of military power.

With a single, loud "Damn," Zuckschwerdt ordered full speed ahead and a concurrent full turn back into the welcome protection of the storm bank. The *Cormoran* responded immediately and heeled over, to the great discomfort of the entire crew, back into the murky squall. From its fringe the Germans observed the ominous foe. The *Satsuma* was on a direct course toward the *Cormoran* and could obviously blow her out of the water with barely shifting a gun. As they waited helplessly for the first, devastating shells, the alert wireless operator reported that the radio sounds from the *Satsuma* continued without interruption, a probable sign that they had not seen the *Cormoran*. Within a brief time the *Satsuma* turned away from both the island and the German ship. For a second time the enemy's inability to maintain an effective watch spared the tiny raider. Zuckschwerdt made haste to move away for the barely discernible horizon. Three quarters of an hour later, the darkness was complete. Dinner was a welcome meal after the brief, but shattering, tension of the earlier encounter. For many it was the moment to learn about the entire affair since those crew members below decks had no awareness of the events.

Now that Yap was occupied by the enemy, Zuckschwerdt changed his course for the Caroline Islands. He had to find a place to hide the *Cormoran* while also seeking coal. Unfortunately the possibilities were quite limited. Of necessity the eventual anchorage had to be near a cable or wireless station free of enemy control. The sole neutral harbor in the area was Guam, the most southerly of the Marianas, which belonged to the United States. From a visit in 1913 Zuckschwerdt knew that the Americans could not provide sufficient coal for his needs, but the cable station might perhaps be used to locate colliers elsewhere. He could not, however, expect to use it without alerting the enemy as to his exposed location and, in the event the Americans did not provide access to the station, his coal supply would really be exhausted. Given this circumstance, he deemed it advisable to send a boat to Guam manned by officers who knew the American post from their previous visit. They might be able to send off various messages through friends from that time. He needed, however, both a boat and a place of concealment.

Once more Zuckschwerdt's excellent memory and previous service in the protectorates paid handsome dividends. Even as the *Cormoran* fled Yap, he assembled his immediate officers for a careful review session. The point of his remarks was to underscore their desperate situation. By listening to various communication stations, the ship's wireless personnel had pinpointed numerous enemy ships and had accepted as fact the Japanese or Australian occupation of the German colonies. Without coal and surrounded by the foe, the *Cormoran* could not attempt any military action. She was powerless despite her enlarged crew, efficient guns, and high morale. Zuckschwerdt then submitted to his listeners that they needed to seek a proper hideaway and send a boat to Guam for aid. He suggested that they use the lagoon of Lamotrek Island in the West Carolines, about 380 miles south of Guam. It was off the natural traffic route, yet close enough to the wide ocean expanses to permit an immediate escape attempt. Shaped roughly like a triangle, the lagoon provided a superlative hiding place. Although not high—only 1 to 1.5 meters for the most part —and not overly large—less than 400 meters wide—the main island offered some cover by its natural vegetation. There were about 250 natives and an English trader who owned a small boat. The area had been visited only once in recent years, by the old *Cormoran* in 1913. Once again Zuckschwerdt's carefully thought out arguments precluded the need to use his command prerogatives. Everyone fell in with the captain's thought, and he soon had the ship moving toward Lamotrek.

On October 12 the *Cormoran* slipped into the lagoon and dropped anchor as close in to the main island as possible. Immediately the curious English trader, Henry Simms, came on board to meet his unexpected visitors. He knew nothing of the war and listened avidly to the German version of hostilities. After a brief exchange he agreed to sell his cutter, the *Ocean Comber*, of some eight tons, to the Germans for a mutually satisfactory price. As important he accepted as well a proposal by Zuckschwerdt to influence the natives in favor of the Germans. As a cosmopolitan, married to a native girl, he saw no reason to carry on the war alone. The Germans attempted to seal the bargain with a magnificent tropical jacket which one of the ship's officers had carefully saved from Tsingtao. This gift had little effect on the island ruler, but the news that Japan was in the war against Germany had a telling impact. Some years earlier, Simms reported, a Japanese merchant had resided in Lamotrek and had taken constant advantage of him. He would do anything to keep the "Yellow Peril" from his somewhat confined shores.

With Simms's outright support, Zuckschwerdt personally supervised the preparation of the *Ocean Comber* for the long trip to Guam. The following day three officers and five New Guineans started off on their dubious voyage to Guam under the leadership of Lt. Hubert Frank. If all went well, they would arrive in the American harbor in fourteen days, and posing as South Pacific traders seeking a healthful change of climate. Once ashore they would divide assignments and visit old friends still resident on the island. The *Cormoran* had paid a five-day visit to Guam in 1913, and many of the same people would probably still be there. With the connivance of these people, they would try to send out cables in every direction seeking food and coal. After a brief wait for possible answers, the group would meet again and search out a way back to Lamotrek. Hopefully they could use the *Ocean Comber*, but, failing that, they would find other means. The eight uncertain sailors received a cheerful send-off and disappeared over a serenely calm, blue sea.

Zuckschwerdt, in the European custom, waved patiently until they were a small speck near the skyline, and then turned to his new station. The first order was security. He insisted upon a continuous lookout post, twenty-four-hour wireless watch, and a careful, if inconspicuous, count of native canoe traffic. Above all he had to keep his haven a secret from the outside world. Within a few days Zuckschwerdt discovered that his concerns about the natives were unnecessary. They could not move eastward, because their canoes were ill-equipped to combat the strong equatorial current. The western and northern islands in the area were too far away for the small canoes, which could not store sufficient water and food for the journey. Beyond their geographic isolation, however, the natives gave no reason to suspect their motives. Two days after the *Cormoran*'s arrival, Simms invited the entire crew to the favorite native entertainment, a "sing along." Zuckschwerdt ransacked the entire ship for appropriate presents and appointed responsible individuals to make certain that every native received something. Everyone enjoyed himself at the affair, and the exchange provided a firm base for future relations. Thereafter the two groups maintained an active social life together with boat races, swimming contests, and costume parties. The genial joviality of all participants assured a pleasant social life far from both war and civilization.

Along with such delightful diversions, Zuckschwerdt understood the need to keep his crew prepared for both action and immediate departure. His chief challenge was to protect the sailors from the constant tropical lure of lethargy. Without the omnipresent uncertainty of encountering the enemy, the men would soon surrender to the native existence. Zuckschwerdt, refusing to accept this possibility, moved against it before anyone else thought about the problem. He integrated the *Planet*'s crew into his own ship's routine as participants rather than as volunteer marines. Likewise he personally supervised all their exercises every day. Again he was constantly present, whether at the calisthenics which opened each morning or at the surprise drills he used to maintain vigilance. For the remaining hours in the day he kept the crew occupied with a host of activities.

They had to make or find everything necessary to maintain the ship and keep it in proper working condition. All fresh water came from rainwater, caught in tubs and pans as well as wide pits dug on the atoll itself. In addition some usable cooking water was won by digging holes on the main island. Work parties washed down the ship each day with seawater, using brushes and brooms made from palm leaf ribs. To expedite both control and efficiency, Zuckschwerdt had the crew divided into subdivisions. Twice each day one of these subordinate groups left the ship for the land taking its laundry with it. On shore they received homemade soap produced through a continuing series of experiments. It contained a measure of sand, which irritated both skin and tempers, and possessed a peculiar odor previously unknown to the men. Once they had completed their toilet and laundry the sailors carried back water and supplies gathered and produced by another party. There was always a period of two hours when no one was permitted near the German research station. In their search for soaps, substitute foods, beers, and so forth, the amateur chemists often blew up their rough quarters. While no one was ever seriously hurt, the sight of flying equipment accompanied by an explosion was not an uncommon event.

Aboard ship one boiler had to be kept heated for cooking and maintaining the fire-fighting equipment. Since coal was far too important for this use wood had to be substituted as much as possible. The engineers could add coal to the wood only when the steam pressure fell below minimal standards. For cutting wood

Zuckschwerdt stationed a work detail of twenty to thirty men on another island in the lagoon, some four miles from the ship. This assignment was the least desirable assignment and the men abhorred the duty roster published each day.

While the hard labor under a broiling sun was unpleasant, one could endure it. The insect life, however, made the day a true hell. The variety and assortment would have provided a lifelong paradise for the entomologist, but, for laboring sailors, the tiny bugs were almost intolerable. A particularly offensive mite ruled supreme as the most frightening enemy. It was small enough to escape all but the most minute investigation and quickly burrowed under the skin causing a painful, festering sore. Men often had most of their exposed skin—and the hot sun made cover uncomfortable—covered with these wounds. Recovery was a long, drawn-out, patience-exhausting affair.

Once the trees were down, the most punishing physical labor began. The high surf on the reefs surrounding the lagoon prevented easy transportation of the logs. The men required hours each day simply to get the wood past the boiling waves to the free water and the bobbing ship's boats. At the beginning the ship's motorboat hauled these boats through the water, but with the exhaustion of the gasoline supply, the men had to row the wood to the ship.

Food remained a continuously serious problem because no one, including the captain, knew how long the stay might last. Zuckschwerdt, as a protective device, instituted food rationing within a few days of their arrival. The supplies on hand were not extensive, and meals grew progressively smaller. There were flour, beans, peas, coffee and tea, and some salted, rancid meat left from the *Rjasan*. Efforts to supplement this diet with the abundant variety of fish available proved largely abortive since the catching was more difficult than the observing. The coral reefs made the use of nets impossible, reducing the crew to angling with crude weapons—hook and line, hands, and rifles. The art of tropical angling was not simple, and it required considerable skill to catch fish in the textbook manner. Only a few persistent or experienced fishermen eventually mastered the skill. Likewise the Germans found it most difficult to emulate the natives, who employed spears with considerable dexterity. Many volunteers sought to enjoy the sport of shooting fish. A good rifleman could kill large fish with ease, and the New Guineans enjoyed diving for the spoil. But the sport required great patience and the return was often more valuable for morale than food value. When possible the Germans purchased foodstuffs from the natives. This meant an occasional duck, chicken, small pig, or, on a rare occasion, an errant turtle. The natives had very little themselves, however, and disliked trading or selling animals, because they represented real wealth. Eggs were always very small and, laid in the bushes, were difficult to see under the best of circumstances. As a bulk supplement Zuckschwerdt started, in November, to purchase coconuts from the natives at three pennies each. This action demanded careful negotiations with Simms, who feared the disruption of his isolated economy. Eventually the Germans ordered some 700 a day. The milk was used for drinking and as a cooking aid, the butter and lard having disappeared shortly after the ship's arrival. All the coconut meat was consumed in its raw form or used as a mash base for other substances. For drinks the crew had only tea and coconut milk. To combat the heat these liquids were cooled by lowering them to the bottom of the sea, a distance of some thirty-five meters. The pressure often forced the corks to give way. While the loss of drink was not so disastrous, the effect on morale was not pleasant when an individual lost his chance for a cooling draught. In such fashion the Cormoran's crew passed its time.

Throughout the stay at Lamotrek, Zuckschwerdt's essential concern remained the fear of destruction or capture by the enemy. He had the wireless moved ashore and demanded a constant watch. By consistent reporting, plotting, and recording, the radiomen soon located the shipping patterns around them. The Japanese had eight ships moving through the Carolines. They remained, with a few notable exceptions, close to the major islands, but met at regular intervals at a point not too distant from Lamotrek. At such times one or more steamers could be heard, which Zuckschwerdt surmised indicated a food and coal supply point.

Everyone grew accustomed to this traffic, until November 6, when the bored lookout suddenly screamed a warning. A Japanese steamer, without any wireless noise, moved past the atoll, her masts, funnels, and personnel clearly discernible to the wary, concealed Germans. Because of her wood fire the Cormoran fortunately developed only a very fine, scarcely noticeable smoke, and her masts, surely visible to a vigilant observer, remained obscured by the coconut trees and vegetation. At first the eager Zuckschwerdt thought seriously about trying to capture the Japanese vessel, but ultimately decided against it. Heating the boilers required time, and leaving the lagoon demanded a movement in the opposite direction. The time loss made pursuit a risky affair at great cost to the *Cormoran*'s limited coal supply. Since the estimated speed of the Japanese vessel approximated that of the *Cormoran*, pursuit was a chancy affair at best. If the Germans failed to catch their quarry, the sole alternative was to go on to Guam, because the limited coal supply would preclude returning to Lamotrek.

Two days later Zuckschwerdt learned that he had made a fortunate decision against pursuit. A canoe from Latuval Island, about forty miles east of Lamotrek, brought a letter from a German trader resident there. A Japanese warship had waited several days by his island for a steamship. Once it arrived, they both had departed to the east. Trying to capture the vessel would have been fatal for the *Cormoran*. While relieved over this information concerning his good luck, Zuckschwerdt yet found the letter a disturbing note. Other people now knew about his location, which could prove eminently dangerous. He therefore ordered one of his officers to ride the canoe back to Latuval to collect more details on the natives there and to instruct his German friend about influencing the natives.

The connection from Latuval to Lamotrek by sail canoe was very fast because of the equatorial current in that direction. On the other hand, the return trip with the opposing current was very slow, and no one envied the officer sent back, despite the change in scenery. After two days his canoe remained visible to Lamotrek. A week later he returned with the good news that no one need fear the circulation of news about their location. The German resident, a naval reservist, had complete authority over the area and suffered little interference from the Japanese. Zuckschwerdt sent back instructions via the native paddlers ordering him to serve as an intelligence collector rather than activating him for service with the *Cormoran*. Thereafter Zuckschwerdt demanded much closer attention to both visual and wireless observation. In this way the Germans learned of Tsingtao's fall, the *Emden*'s fate, and the sea battles of Coronel and the Falkland Islands. They were definitely alone.

Each week merged into another, some with more tension, some with less. The trade winds arrived in November, bringing many odd-shaped clouds. On the horizon these clouds made adequate observation very difficult. Only the keenest observer could distinguish between cloud and smoke. As a result many false alarms relieved the monotony. Equally the stars often radiated a color and shape akin to a ship's lantern, disturbing many watchers. The helpful natives, with their many fantasies, were often taken in by these natural tricks and frequently reported shadowy funnels behind the lights.

By the end of November the pressures from island isolationism began to reach unbearable limits. Lamotrek was not the tropical paradise of cheap pulp romances, but a dirty, disagreeable island. The food was not enough to more than line empty stomachs; the daily chores not enough to maintain adequate morale. Everything was fast running out. As the paper necessities for daily existence were exhausted, the ship's library began to disappear—only a worn copy of international military regulations was declared essential. On November 17 a surveyor from the *Planet*, Helmut Glaser, died of typhoid fever. His comrades buried him with full military honors and erected a rock cairn memorial for him. His passing created a melancholy mood which grew each day. Zuckschwerdt, seeing this pensive attitude, gave up all hope for the success of his Guam expedition and assumed that something had gone awry with the *Ocean Comber*. He decided, then, to try to capture the next Japanese vessel to come by and, if he was unsuccessful, to go on to Guam. With luck he might find a way to persuade the Americans to disgorge some coal and leave before the Allies cut off the port.

During the night of November 27 the wireless receiver buzzed with a loud reception from a nearby vessel. Zuckschwerdt ordered the boilers heated, but the unknown ship moved away before the *Cormoran* could get under way. The same thing happened again on December 4. On December 12, with food supplies fast approaching the final crumbs, the wireless revealed an approaching Japanese warship. Zuckschwerdt decided to risk everything and ordered the ship prepared for both the sea and immediate combat.

As he was about to move away, however, the lookout reported that natives had ignited the huge fires used to both light the way and to give welcome to visiting canoes. He held up the final orders to see about possible news from another island. The next morning Simms arrived at an early hour. His obvious excitement and patent concern heralded a significant report: Simms reported that canoes from Truk had appeared the previous night. They had sailed the 350 miles from Truk in four days, bringing news that the Japanese had turned that island into a complete naval station. There were eight big ships, several torpedo boats, and one lonely submarine. A crew had landed several cannon, while the admiral in charge had informed the natives that he intended to stay for a long, long time. He had added the thought that other Japanese vessels would soon hoist the national flag on other islands. Zuckschwerdt needed no more. He concluded that the wireless activity came from a Japanese cruiser which could be headed in only one direction, Lamotrek. With intense urgency he dispatched a boat to the wood-cutting island to pick up the work party and ordered the anchor lifted at noon on December 12.

Under the circumstances farewells were brief, and at least three known romances ended with tearful good-byes. The Germans left their crude installations intact as a present to Simms. Zuckschwerdt told the Englishman that he was taking the *Cormoran* to Manila but did not expect the inland ruler to be taken in by the ruse. That city was some 1,700 miles distant, and the denuded wood island provided mute testimony to the ship's fuel problems. If luck held, however, the Japanese might lose a few hours' time before reaching the obvious answer.

Under the press of assumed pursuit, Zuckschwerdt ordered the most direct route to Guam. To supplement the uncertain coal resources the ship had a goodly supply of coconut husks. Zuckschwerdt also had all the furniture earmarked according to priority. En route the coconuts disappeared, but most of the ship's furnishings survived the ordeal. As the ship pounded along, Zuckschwerdt considered his approach. The entrance to Apra Harbor in Guam was on the west side of the island and he assumed that the Japanese would definitely have a patrol vessel on watch. In addition he thought the correct Americans would give him only twenty-four hours to complete his activities, a circumstance putting a great premium on time.

The *Cormoran* made Guam during the night of December 13, and Zuckschwerdt took her to the eastern shoreline, which was free of reefs and very steep. It offered excellent protection against the elements and possible enemy surprise. As they hove to for the night, the wireless operator reported an open exchange between the American harbor guard ship and the land station that a Japanese warship was visible on the western horizon. At dawn's first light Zuckschwerdt moved the *Cormoran* at full power around the island, remaining as close to the coastline as he dared, and darted into the harbor. While the crew strained their eyes from their battle stations, no one saw the expected Japanese warship. Once inside the *Cormoran* reduced her speed to avoid unduly alarming the defenses. As she moved slowly toward the inner bay the observant crew noted the *Ocean Comber* blocked up on the beach. She was not a happy sight. Clearly the crew had not achieved their goals.

Chapter 5   Death

The *Cormoran* passed the outer edge of the harbor at 8:40 A.M. at full speed. The engine room crew had tied down the safety valves on her boilers in order to extract every possible ounce of energy from her flailing engine. En route Zuckschwerdt dispatched a wireless message addressed to the governor, "*Cormoran* asks for allowance of entering port in the deficiency of coal and provisions." Although the message was not phrased in the most felicitous English, the intent was clear. Navy Capt. William J. Maxwell, the resident governor, granted the simple plea. The *Cormoran* dropped anchor at 11:15. Zuckschwerdt immediately asked for an interview with Maxwell to state his problems and to set forth certain requests. The governor agreed to the meeting and Zuckschwerdt, with another officer, quickly accepted an automobile ride to the American's official residence. In his undue haste, he ran to the building in the most undignified fashion but, thereafter, he followed strict military procedure in terms of saluting, extending apologies for the imposition, and standing at rigid attention. At the same time he did not waste a moment beyond the necessary protocol statements. Zuckschwerdt stated that he had just come from the South Seas, that he was extremely short of fuel (having less than 50 tons of coal left in the ship's bunkers) and provisions, and that he requested sufficient coal (a minimum of 1,500 tons) and foodstuffs to reach German East Africa.

Maxwell responded with a few words of understanding for his visitor's unhappy predicament and his appreciation for Zuckschwerdt's command of English. But he then clearly stated that Guam could not provide more than 200 tons of coal and provisions for thirty days. The island storehouses could not spare more without severely curtailing the resources of the civilian populace.

He, therefore, had to hold the Germans accountable under the international rules governing such cases. Zuckschwerdt had the alternatives of departing within twenty-four hours or of interning his ship for the duration of hostilities. The meeting was most correct in terms of protocol and proper usage, but the resolution was abundantly clear to all the participants. Maxwell, for his own reasons, would not give sufficient material support to allow the Germans any hope for survival on the open sea. Zuckschwerdt expressed his appreciation for Maxwell's consideration, said goodbye, smartly saluted, and hastily departed for his ship.

On the way back to the *Cormoran* he asked the accompanying American officer about the fate of his advance party in *Ocean Comber*. His guide replied that the tiny cutter, virtually filled with water from a difficult trip, had limped into port on October 28. The naval personnel who met them in the harbor had immediately recognized one of the exhausted officers and reported the fact to their commanding officer. Confronted almost immediately with this accusation, the bone-weary Germans had readily admitted their national allegiance. To their credit, at the same time, they refused to reveal the *Cormoran*'s location. Instead, they brazenly demanded the right to cable San Francisco for coal and supplies. Maxwell had refused outright to even consider the request and, following the normal one-day delay, had interned them. One of the officers, Lt. Hans Muller, had endeavored to conceal his true identity by asserting that he was the German high commissioner for Papua and was, therefore, entitled to diplomatic treatment. His ploy had almost succeeded. Had a suitable vessel been passing through, the United States Department of State was willing to grant him passage to Manila. Without available transportation, however, his actual status was soon discovered and he joined his comrades as an internee. Thereafter the entire group had been living with the station complement on a daily allowance (five dollars for officers, one dollar for the New Guineans) in a style well beyond that provided by their sea quarters. They had received the virtual run of the island as well as accommodations through the aid of a sympathetic German family ("Die blaue Bude").

Back on board ship Zuckschwerdt revealed the substance of the Maxwell conversations to his assembled officers. Although obviously upset and more than a little angry over the American intransigence, he fully understood the rationale behind it. In a few words the captain explained that the *Cormoran* could not carry on the war under such uncertain circumstances. This time he had no alternative and must intern the ship for what he hoped would not be a long time. On December 15, at 10:00 A.M. he agreed to internment in Guam, and he provided a roster of the personnel, which now included 33 officers, 307 men, 4 Chinese, and 29 South Sea Islanders. Concurrently he requested the return of the *Ocean Comber's* crew from their semiluxurious shore internment. Maxwell readily agreed, and the internees promptly rejoined their friends, with obviously mixed emotions.

Immediately after receiving Zuckschwerdt's commitment, Maxwell ordered Lt. Comdr. M. G. Cook to draw up the internment conditions. The governor insisted that the Germans remove various parts of their armament to make them inoperative, remain quartered on the *Cormoran*, and agree not to go beyond a carefully determined boundary line when on shore. Since Apra Harbor was not overly well protected against the elements, Maxwell proposed to keep the ship's machinery in operative condition. If weather conditions became so serious as to threaten the ship's safety, Zuckschwerdt should take her out of the harbor to the open sea. For this eventuality Maxwell proposed to keep 200 tons of coal aboard the *Cormoran*, while Zuckschwerdt must pledge himself not to move the ship without the express permission of the governor.

Given the alternative, Zuckschwerdt had no possible choice and accepted the conditions. Even as he agreed to the brief document, the Japanese cruiser, *Iwate*, appeared at the harbor entrance. Her captain, Vice Admiral Matsumura, asked if a German auxiliary cruiser had entered the harbor. The *Iwate* had come directly from Lamotrek, where Simms had told them about the *Cormoran's* sojourn there, hasty departure, and probable destination. He had proved again the fickle loyalties of island "monarchs." Maxwell gave the Japanese a full explanation of *Cormoran's* history as he knew it and the cruiser departed for the Carolines. Her impressive presence made the Germans aware of their indebtedness to the natives for their early warning, and indicated the timeliness of Zuckschwerdt's decision to remain in Guam.

Then the *Cormoran's* crew settled down to their internment, a period which was to last much longer than anyone anticipated at the time. The hours and days passed on two levels; one the formal relationships with the legal authorities in Guam and Washington, the other the personal, direct level with their fellow crewmen and the local populace. The first was confined largely to the power struggle between Zuckschwerdt and Maxwell, with the crew more interested observers than active participants. This conflict of wills began almost immediately after the two men accepted and signed the internment documents.

Captain Maxwell had only recently arrived to assume control of the island. He had officially taken over on March 29, 1914. Within a few weeks he began to show signs of mental deterioration, which included a severe megalomania with certain religious overtones. At the time of the *Cormoran*'s arrival he was deeply suspicious of all human motives and refused to participate in open, direct exchange with anyone. Since these fears extended to his own subordinates, communication was extraordinarily difficult. He kept his own confidences and issued independent orders, often contradictory in nature. He gave these instructions at odd hours and orally, which made confirmation difficult, if not impossible. His mistrust and fears manifested themselves in a host of irregular, unpleasant, and incomprehensible actions. When a local merchant visited the governor with a request Maxwell replied in a highly negative manner which elicited an immediate protest: "But sir, what you have proposed is against international law." Maxwell responded with even greater force, "I am the law, I make the law, I break the law. My powers here are equal to those of the Kaiser himself, and are exceeded only by those of the Pope."

As a Catholic, Maxwell practiced a diverse set of religious principles. He would often attend every mass on a given Sunday while not participating in a single one on other Sundays. On one occasion he sent a messenger to the church to ask the priest not to ring the bells calling the faithful to service. As the confused priest contemplated this strange request, a nearby native tied a rope to the bell ringing system, and, walking a short distance away, rang the bells like a claxon. The angry governor sent an investigating party without success and dispatched an intemperate note to the innocent priest.

Maxwell's unfortunate mental state was not helped by Zuckschwerdt, who always insisted upon correct behavior and slavish adhesion to protocol. Since Zuckschwerdt's command of the English idiom was virtually perfect and he had saved all the copies of international laws and practices from untimely destruction in Lamotrek, he was in a position to bring severe pressure upon the sorely tormented Maxwell. Within a few weeks the relations between the two men reached a strained point where they simply stopped seeing each other. They put all communications, no matter how picayune, on paper and undertook a basic, undeclared personal war against each other.

The first confrontation occurred shortly after the *Cormoran* dropped her internment anchor in Apra Harbor. As soon as the news of her arrival reached Washington, D.C., the German ambassador, Johann Graf von Bernstorff, asked the American secretary of state, William Jennings Bryan, to forward $25,000 to the *Cormoran*. The money was for Zuckschwerdt's use in meeting the living expenses in Guam. Again unfortunately, the American diplomats promptly lost the communication and sacrificed two days to searching for it. On December 19 they had to admit defeat and to ask for a carbon copy. Not until December 21 did the money go forward by cable to Guam. Unfortunately the cablegram could not provide the funds directly but authorized Maxwell to transfer the money to the Germans if he had sufficient financial resources on hand. If not, he should provide a reasonable amount for the Germans. The governor had only a limited sum directly under his control and Guam did not possess a single bank. He decided that $5,000 was sufficient to meet German requirements. His judgment was made without consultation and without explanation to anyone. In a written note to Zuckschwerdt, Maxwell stated that the remaining money would be forthcoming in February, when the American supply vessel, *Supply*, returned from a lengthy trip to Manila.

For Zuckschwerdt the economic question was of secondary importance. Far more significant was the direct issue of arbitrary decision making and the total lack of even a cursory explanation. He rose to the occasion with a vehement protest against Maxwell's cavalier, high-handed attitude. It was, he said, against the rules of war, against human dignity, and against the simple rules of maritime usage. Zuckschwerdt's protest was an unorthodox but effective declaration of war between two strong-willed men. Although placed within the limits imposed by neutrality, this personal struggle had all the signs of open conflict.

Before the two protagonists could set down the delimiting lines of their battleground a new incident triggered additional trouble. In early January 1915 the German consul at Manila sent Zuckschwerdt a brief cable in cipher. Maxwell simply refused to permit its delivery. He insisted that he have written assurance that the contents were innocuous and a statement summarizing the message itself. This time the German Embassy in Washington lodged a formal protest, while concurrently informing Zuckschwerdt of the action. The latter sent off another angry note to Maxwell, which the governor refused to either accept or acknowledge in any way. The subject of concern was not, he claimed, within Zuckschwerdt's official knowledge. The German, thoroughly incensed, dispatched an equally intemperate missive to his foe. In it he accused the American official of personal hatred and professional incompetence. He used terms scarcely conducive to bridging the chasm between the two men.

On January 16 the American State Department overruled the governor and ordered that the *Cormoran* captain might receive ciphered messages without interruption. Having won both a moral and tactical victory in this paper combat, Zuckschwerdt pushed his advantage. On January 31 he submitted a brief note in cipher, together with a terse abstract of its contents, to Maxwell for transmission to Washington. When he received the anticipated curt refusal, he sent off an immediate message to the German ambassador citing the previous procedural ruling. This time the American bureaucrats ruled in favor of Maxwell. The Germans could receive but not send messages in code. In fact, the ruling went on, the outgoing communications would have to be submitted in English. The governor dispatched a short note to the ship, without an addressee, announcing his victory.

In February both men attempted new tactical measures. With his money tied up Zuckschwerdt sought to gain financial freedom. He solicited approval for purchasing materials in San Francisco and shipping them to Guam on American vessels. Maxwell recommended against this unwarranted use of his country's shipping space in support of an interned warship but lost the decision. The Washington officials agreed to let Zuckschwerdt spend his money in San Francisco. To make matters even more disturbing the Navy Department agreed that the U.S.S. *Supply* might transport goods from Manila for the Germans. She made quarterly trips for Guam and, as Navy Secretary Josephus Daniels stated, could accommodate various items for the interned ship. He also added his permission for Zuckschwerdt's use of the War Department's monthly transport service between California and Manila, the vessels calling at Guam both coming and going.

Maxwell did not appreciate this obvious rebuff and, when a case of typhoid appeared on the *Cormoran*, he confined the crew to strict quarantine for a month. The ship's medical personnel had to cope with the disease with their own resources. While their prompt attention prevented any deaths, the governor's lack of concern did not endear him to the angry men. Concurrently he sought to prevent the Germans from ordering liquors, beers, or other bonded goods from the customs officers in San Francisco without paying the requisite custom duties. Again Zuckschwerdt won when the Washington authorities agreed to allow the withdrawal of such goods without paying the normal tariff charges.

With the German navy winning so many "battles" Maxwell, not in the least well, had to find another recourse for his frustrations. On January 27, the birthday of Kaiser Wilhelm II, the governor did not participate in any way nor did he permit any other vessel to take part in the celebration festivities. As a token notice he sent a junior officer who was, in accordance with the governor's specific instructions, not arrayed in the full dress uniform normally demanded by the occasion. This calculated insult had its desired effect upon Zuckschwerdt who lost his temper once more and in direct, strident terms lodged a harsh protest of the most powerful nature with the American secretary of state. Maxwell tried to disarm his unwanted, testy visitor with the injunction that the status of the *Cormoran* as a warship was not clearly established and that the Americans did not need to follow customary protocol. Zuckschwerdt seized upon this flimsy excuse to demand an examination of his ship's status and the fundamental right of the United States to intern her. Maxwell sent the note to Washington without comment and suffered for his oversight. While Secretary of State Bryan had overlooked Zuckschwerdt's direct protest, he responded promptly that no one entertained the slightest doubts concerning the *Cormoran*'s military position as a warship. At the same time he made an oblique apology for the Guam administrator to the German captain.

Given this minor victory and the numerous other painful, petty exchanges, Zuckschwerdt moved toward flanking action. On April 4 he wrote Graf von Bernstorff about the *Cormoran*. As reasons for his anger Zuckschwerdt pointed out the imminent arrival of the typhoon season, the need to dock the ship for needed repairs, and the growing psychological pressures on the men after so long a stay in the tropics. Since the *Supply* would sail for San Francisco at the end of the month, he proposed that she convoy the raider across the Pacific to the Golden Gate. Bernstorff immediately asked the American secretary of state for a ruling. He, in turn, requested a judgment from the Joint State and Navy Neutrality Board. After a hasty deliberation the board responded, on April 14, that they foresaw no objection to shifting the *Cormoran* so long as the crew provided a parole of honorable activity during the transfer. They also thought that the German government should agree to the American right to transfer the ship without changing her interned status in any way.

This time the Navy Department proved more recalcitrant and refused to accept this reading of the problem. It replied that the movement might bring complications with other powers, impose major responsibilities upon the *Supply*, which was not well equipped to meet them, and force Guam to give up personnel which it could ill afford to lose at the time. In addition, Maxwell emphasized the limited supply of coal on Guam and the tenuous state of the island's defenses. To outfit the *Cormoran* would seriously curtail the available supplies on hand and demand immediate replacement at a time when the navy had serious difficulty in meeting such needs at all outlying stations. The military strength on Guam could not afford the dispatch of men to the mainland. In addition to regular garrison duty, the marines were involved with the Insular Patrol, an early type of Peace Corps in which selected soldiers received civilian assignments in support of the native populace. In general they lived with the people, sought out their needs, and endeavored to help them in every way. To withdraw essential manpower would thus cripple the program which had just started and leave the island without a semblance of defense.

In the middle of this controversy the State Department wavered momentarily between the two choices. The final push to a decision came from the Russian Embassy. The ambassador, George Bakkmetoof, wrote on April 30, to question whether the *Cormoran* should be considered a Russian or a German vessel. He expressed serious concern over the fact that a competent German prize court had never adjudicated the question of her seizure. In view of this fact, that is, that no German court had condemned the *Rjasan*, he thought that she remained Russian property, and he asked that the *Rjasan* be returned to her rightful owner. The American response was quick and directly to the point. The *Rjasan* had been taken and used by the Germans. She was a warship and could not be admitted to any other identity. This service assured her treatment as a warship. At the same time, the State Department sent off a terse denial to Zuckschwerdt's request for the change to San Francisco. They could not afford any further controversy on a delicate interpretation. The information came to Zuckschwerdt through a gleeful Maxwell's messenger, certainly ample revenge for the old *Rjasan*.

Having garnered at least a partial victory, Maxwell moved to contain his adversary even more. In July he asked the Navy Department to renew the question of cipher messages. This time the governor was considerably more clever than during his earlier attempt to halt the message exchange. He asked that all communications for or to the *Cormoran* be sent through the Navy Department and be transmitted in English, subject to official censorship. Secretary Daniels reviewed the issue with detailed caution, but he finally accepted the idea. Henceforth no coded messages could be accepted from or delivered to the *Cormoran* unless they appeared in English. Concurrently Maxwell enjoined the Germans from receiving news from the German consul in Honolulu, Hawaii. He had found that Zuckschwerdt often had details of significant international events before he himself had any inkling of them. Since Guam received precious little general information over the cable, the Americans depended upon the monthly mail calls for world news. Again his injunction received the sustaining authority of the Navy Department, thereby increasing Zuckschwerdt's anger while further reducing his independence.

In September Zuckschwerdt tried again to obtain a transfer to a cooler climate. This new plea used three cases of insanity, a case of tuberculosis, various other tropical diseases, and the dangerous harbor conditions for support. Maxwell, as was expected, vetoed the entire proposal, and his navy superiors confirmed his ruling. The decision marked the end of the major battles between the two men but initiated a new variety of minor skirmishes. They entered into serious word struggles over the right of the ship's complement to invest in German war loans, the crew's participation in social events, the methods best employed for riding out storms, the transfer of money, shifting mentally ill crew members to the United States, and various other concerns of protocol. These verbal conflicts were always harsh, always bitter, and always fought to a decision. Maxwell, because of his official position, won the majority of them, but he always had to fight hard for victory.

The struggle continued into 1916 without relief. In February Zuckschwerdt renewed his plea for permission to shift his ship to another harbor. He had, by this time, largely used up his stock of reasons and explanations. In 1916 he contented himself with the simple observation that the tropical sea animals had made serious inroads into the *Cormoran*'s hull—to the point that she was no longer seaworthy. Maxwell's negative response and the concurrence of the Navy Department were old, dispiriting, known tales for the hardy Zuckschwerdt.

On February 27, 1916, there was much greater excitement. A small American marine group, en route to its training area, observed a scarred man enjoying an outing with a local girl and her family. They decided that the unknown person must belong to the Germans and that he was well over the decreed demarcation line. The leader reported the matter through channels to Maxwell. He immediately assumed that the unknown figure could only be Lieutenant Dr. Gebhard, the former district official in Friedrich Wilhelm's Harbor. Maxwell then wrote a stinging formal charge to Zuckschwerdt, in which he directly accused Gebhard of the violation while adding a general comment that the Germans had consistently broken the internment rules. Zuckschwerdt promptly filed an equally insulting response damning what he termed an unfounded slur on his men and their honor. The exchanges grew progressively more heated until Maxwell finally refused even to sign them. In the end Maxwell gave way for lack of direct evidence in his original charge, but his aide and intermediary, Lt. Comdr. M. G. Cook, wrote in his final note: "The Governor of Guam takes note of the well intended efforts of the Commanding officer of the *Cormoran* toward complying with the spirit as well as the rules of internment and hopes that the efforts to secure amicable relations with the Naval Station of Guam will be extended to include the Government of Guam." The plaintive expression in the communication had little effect upon the intractable German. After protracted investigation, interrogations, and harsh words Maxwell ordered a curfew for all the ship's crew. The crew would be back aboard ship by midnight. The new regulations provided a bitter blow to the Germans who saw the curtailment of their freedom as a first step toward complete isolation. Shortly afterward Maxwell demanded that all group exercises, mostly "hikes," be cleared beforehand and that the number of participants be reported directly to him. These were unfortunate regulations to the crew who enjoyed many friends ashore.

Zuckschwerdt simply refused to give ground on the issue of control in any way. In the end he won the battle of wills. Maxwell, showing the effects of his personal mental problems and the constant stress of dealing with an unwelcome, permanent guest, broke down, and the local doctors agreed that he needed a long-term, carefully administered rest cure. Acting upon this advice the local officers relieved Maxwell. Since relief was immediate, Lt. Comdr. William P. Cronan, the senior officer after Maxwell and commander of the U.S.S. *Supply*, assumed control of the island. Cronan, a far more reasonable and pleasant man, immediately sent his adjutant to the *Cormoran* to report the change in command and invited Zuckschwerdt to afternoon tea. The latter accepted the principle of the suggestion but, ever on guard, insisted that the acting governor was his junior and should first be his guest on the *Cormoran*. Cronan complied with alacrity and spent a pleasant two hours aboard ship. During the course of the exchange he apologized for the numerous inconveniences occasioned by his predecessor and expressed his hope for both better human and official relations.

Despite his friendly beginning and knowledge that his position and authority remained temporary, Cronan insisted upon the total disarmament of the *Cormoran*. While Maxwell had ordered in 1914 that the ship surrender all of its breech mechanisms, he had not asked for the small arms and ammunition. This had been a mistake. Within four hours after giving up the required gun assemblies, the Germans had effectively replaced them with an assortment of workable substitutes. The ship had, then, been an effective warship throughout its internment, fully capable of engaging Guam's ancient armament—a few cannon purchased from a Brazilian ship in 1898. Cronan realized that the sizable German force could do significant damage to the island's defenses. Zuckschwerdt decided not to press his authority, in view of the international situation. The demand was reasonable, understandable, and governed by international law. He fully comprehended his powerful situation but decided against a serious test of strength. In fact, he cooperated in every fashion, effectively giving up all the ship's military hardware.

In return Cronan issued public orders that the Germans were to be treated as friendly guests and that they could enjoy the social life of the island. He also increased the supply of coal for the ship's bunkers to 250 tons and arranged for periodic visits by the chief officers at the naval station to the *Cormoran*, a practice not allowed by Maxwell. These relatively simple changes brought a revolutionary adjustment in the lives of all the persons living in Guam. They shifted the entire framework of relations between Guam and the *Cormoran* from the two-man official struggle to a much more pleasant general social exchange. This adjustment demanded a fundamental change of thought from the difficult Maxwell era where such considerations received very little understanding.

Maxwell, following the original internment, had effectively cut off all social exchange. Because of the governor's attitude, regulations, and general harassment the Germans had no choice but to lead a stringently isolated existence aboard ship. Mixing between the sailors and the inhabitants was controlled as much as possible and the civilians who spoke to any Germans ashore often heard about it from the governor himself. In August 1915 a Mrs. Constable, with three eligible, lonely daughters, had asked permission to invite some German officers to a dinner-dance party. Maxwell rebuffed her design with some cross words about the dubious ancestry of all German officers. Zuckschwerdt subsequently filed a protest over the clearly libelous, colorful terminology but received little satisfaction. The incident did serve to keep the two groups, German and American, fairly well apart. No one was willing or able to challenge Maxwell's ultimate control over everyone. Guam was a long way from the mainland.

Thereafter a series of weather conditions served to create a number of minor adjustments. Often it was impossible for the sailors to return to the *Cormoran* because of darkness, a sudden storm, or official employment ashore. Mechanical difficulties or simple human failure likewise interrupted daily movement. Under such conditions even the difficult Maxwell had to accept the reality of human existence and he finally permitted the Germans to rent a house for overnight stays. This house gradually allowed the exchange of mutual greetings between the two sides and the more adventuresome soon went beyond that level. Throughout they risked and often incurred Maxwell's wrath which was a known legend to everyone. His continued antagonism inhibited the vast majority from undertaking any untoward activity. While everyone despised Maxwell few would chance antagonizing him.

This difficult situation forced some unpleasant realities upon Zuckschwerdt and his crew. They continued merely to exist aboard their ship. After varying periods of tropical service, followed by the weeks of nerve-wracking uncertainty in war, Guam provided no real hope for ultimate survival. To the men the sight of the island became a lure, a psychological goal far beyond its intrinsic value. Zuckschwerdt, continuously facing his blood foe, Maxwell, had the additional problem of keeping his bored men busy with continued drill, abandon ship exercises, and the necessary but enervating ship cleaning activities. In partial response to his crew's needs he sought to provide more sensual pleasures through the funds advanced by the German government. He purchased exotic delicacies, ample liquor supplies, awnings to cover the entire ship, and extras far beyond most sailors' dreams. Despite his continuous activities, however, the men suffered from "Guamitis." Trying to lead a normal life aboard a confined ship was no simple endeavor.

In April 1915 the first members of the crew showed the mental strain of their confinement. Under escort the first man left for San Francisco and the various professional mental facilities in that area. He was the first of ten. His illness, the required escorts, and the prospects of seeing California quickly attracted others to the advantages of mental instability. The number of disturbed persons increased at an incredible rate, and the local doctors and administrators soon had serious problems differentiating between the truly disturbed and the malingerers seeking a pathway to possible freedom. In at least one case a sailor did successfully make the trip to San Francisco as an insane person and immediately deserted. He made his escape without difficulty and survived to live out his years in the City by the Golden Gate. Even so the months passed with precious little progress or consuming interest. Life became more habit than purpose.

Once Maxwell lost his command, the dreary scene changed almost overnight. Cronan openly permitted exchanges between the *Cormoran* crew and Guam's residents and actively participated in many of them. The new freedom rapidly infected everyone. Dances, beach affairs, dinner parties, costume balls, full-dress formal undertakings, and group singing became commonplace in this isolated area, long resigned to sleepy normality. There was, then, scarcely a day when the lively, new German-American friendship did not have a group activity. These efforts permitted romantic interludes as well between the impressive foreigners and the local daughters. The visitors' continental charms proved most successful, and the first of several marriages soon took place. This heady swirl rapidly overcame the morale problems of a listless existence aboard ship. Zuckschwerdt acquired a small bungalow in Agana, the island's major settlement, and gave small weekly dinner parties. These were always in exquisite taste, with the immaculately attired, handsome, and articulate captain always the gracious host. The change, although not of long duration, was pleasant for everyone.

This grand change did not have a long expectancy. While these newly freed individuals in their remote isolation might play, the fates governing the world decided to cut their pleasure short. Although the tempo of island pleasures and gaiety continued at a feverish pace, the deterioration of German-American diplomatic relations became serious. Zuckschwerdt with his calm external demeanor gave no sign of his personal concern for these changes but his actions indicated his growing understanding of probable American entry into the war. He sold his automobile, surrendered his quarters ashore, and became more attentive to matters aboard ship. Certainly no one noticed his reflective nature until subsequent events recalled his growing pensiveness. Zuckschwerdt did clearly see the changes swirling around the island outpost. For some time no one in Guam paid any attention to the tempo of international affairs.

Late in January 1917 Zuckschwerdt issued a general invitation to a dinner fete on board the *Cormoran*. The affair was the first in many weeks and promised to be an elegant undertaking. A Japanese schooner had recently arrived bearing supplies certain to make the occasion an impressive one. For the small community the event would be the highlight of the new year. Zuckschwerdt scheduled it for February 3 and put his entire crew to work on the festive preparations. On the day of the party, however, Washington broke relations with Germany. The Navy Department then sent off a much garbled cablegram to the recently arrived, permanent governor, Capt. Roy C. Smith. Unfortunately he could not fully understand the purport of the instructions and assumed that he should make certain that the *Cormoran* could not leave port under any circumstances. Smith had also heard the widely circulated rumor that the Germans had been hoarding coal for months in preparation for a surprise departure. Once at sea, the rumor went, they would fall upon unprotected commerce throughout the Pacific.

Smith, like his German guest, was often given to impetuous actions. He sat down directly and wrote a polite note to Zuckschwerdt asking that his representatives, Lt. Owen Bartlett and Lt. William Lafrenz, be allowed to inspect the coal supply on the ship. They carried it to the *Cormoran*, where they received the warmly cordial greeting given to friends of long standing. Around them swirled the final preparations for the evening's festivities. Zuckschwerdt invited them to his cabin which also served as his office and accepted Smith's missive with gracious ease. As he began to peruse its contents, however, his demeanor changed immediately. The smile faded, the muscles in his cheeks hardened, and the warm depths of the eyes faded into unreadable opaqueness. Clearly pleasure had turned into rage. He considered quickly and then declined to let the two men survey his ship's bunkers. The reason for his heated, if barely suppressed, anger came from the questioning of his honor and integrity. He indicated however, that his grounds, put forth with polite but clear firmness, rested upon his extraterritorial rights. The acceptance of the inspection principle was too much for him. Bading his visitors a terse farewell, he ordered a junior officer to escort them back to their boat.

When the two uneasy officers returned to the expectant Smith at his headquarters in Agana it was already early afternoon. The governor, now seriously concerned over what had been little more than a formality, immediately drafted a direct order to the *Cormoran*'s captain, demanding that the latter accept an instant inventory. Concurrently Smith ordered the Marine commander on Guam, Col. T. E. Berkeley, to muster his entire force in order to support the ultimatum. Lieutenant Lafrenz hurried away to obtain the shipping required for the boarding party. His place with Bartlett was taken by Lt. E. B. Woodworth. The concerned Smith even insisted that the two men take a civilian engineer with an accurate tape measure to accurately calculate the amount of coal on the *Cormoran*.

Once the trio had assembled in Smith's office, he ordered them on their way with only a quick word pointing out the need for haste and care. He spoke directly to the point, "Very well, Bartlett, confer with Colonel Berkeley, and go out and take the ship." Additional exchange between the two men elicited Smith's hope that a show of force would suffice. Nonetheless the governor intended to obtain the desired inspection without postponement. Bartlett, in accordance with Smith's directions, hastened to discuss the attack plans with the marines. He found them already clambering into various flat barges, together with two small field-pieces. They would quickly hook on to some tugs for the tow out to the raider. While discussing the various signals, boarding plans, combat possibilities, and postvictory activities with the marines, Bartlett had a number of secondary thoughts. One was for the assault force itself, which gave ample evidence of insecurity and desperation. They were a green, inexperienced lot, liable to shoot without real provocation. At the same time, watching the desperate, determined faces around him, he found the entire affair comical. That morning everyone had been concerned with the dinner party—what to wear, when to arrive, what type of house gift to bring, and so forth. Now he was, only a few hours later, engaged in planning the destruction of the host's establishment. Truly an opéra bouffe!

Nonetheless the two officers and the engineer pushed off to renew their demand with Smith's preemptory orders. Bartlett, in his anxiety, clutched Smith's note in his hand throughout the trip. Zuckschwerdt received them in his cabin with stiff formality. He read the order but immediately responded that it in no way altered his position on the fundamental issue. At the same time he was willing to send a message to the German Embassy in Washington, asking for instructions. To fit action to words, Zuckschwerdt gave Bartlett a copy of his proposed cable to Graf von Bernstorff. Under no circumstances would he grant an inspection without the explicit approval of his superiors.

Returning to shore, Bartlett and Woodworth hurried to Smith, who angrily ordered them to take the ship. Bartlett, conscious now of the curious situation, took his career into his hands and spoke out against such action. He managed to persuade Smith to try a show of force before opening hostilities. Guam could, after all, precipitate war between the two powers, an awesome responsibility. The harried governor yielded to the obvious logic but insisted upon haste, because darkness was almost upon them. The trio, eager to obtain a proper decision, made unusual speed in reaching their motor boat.

When they arrived back aboard the *Cormoran* for the third time, they received a much different reception. Some of Zuckschwerdt's staff officers had arrived just ahead of time, bearing the disturbing news that the Americans seemed on the verge of boarding the ship. They reported the gathering of the marine landing party and the loading of the fieldpieces, clear signs of Smith's determination. The officers' obvious concern and reliability convinced Zuckschwerdt that Smith was in deadly earnest and that his action was not a sudden whim. There was much more to the demands than a Maxwellian show of authority. He therefore quickly gave in to the threat of physical intimidation; Bartlett did not even have to point out the governor's determination. Zuckschwerdt accepted the inspection team, although he did insist upon a preliminary written statement. The quickly assembled document established that the German captain had insisted upon his extraterritorial rights and had yielded only to conditions beyond his control. Both men signed the two copies of the paper and each retained a copy for the official record files.

Thereafter Zuckschwerdt did everything possible to facilitate the inspection. All the ship's charts appeared within a few minutes, the ship's hatches opened with equal facility, and the familiar geniality returned to solve all questions. The American resident engineer, under Woodworth's direction, rapidly took the dimensions of the bunkers, uncovered the ship's bottom in two places, and measured the coal with a long, steel tape measure.

Everything tallied within a few tons of the German reported weight, but, as every professional sailor knew, a good ship always possessed a few extra tons as insurance against emergency. With their determination complete and mission fulfilled the Americans prepared for their departure from the ship.

As they watched the final hatch cover being lowered into place, Bartlett apologized quietly for the day's events and expressed regret over the forced cancellation of the dinner party. The visibly astonished Zuckschwerdt replied instantly, "But of course you are to come to dinner! You have unpleasant duties to perform; I have unpleasant duties to perform; but this need make no difference in our personal relationship. We shall expect you for dinner when it is convenient for you to return."

As the begrimed and weary sailors returned to shore, they observed two Ford automobiles, with brightly dressed women laughing expectantly, arrive at the dock. The happy young ladies paid no attention to the soiled landing party but they complained when the Germans on the dock suggested that, for reasons beyond the captain's control, the party's opening festivities had been put off for one half hour.

Despite the day's frustrations and the party's tardy beginning, it was a resounding success. Everyone coming aboard was met by a white-clad officer demonstrating every traditional naval courtesy. The entire ship was covered with bunting, bowers of gay flowers, strange ferns, and tropical tree blossoms. All the tables carried decorations of greens and orchids formed in the shape of hanging tree flowers. Within this heady atmosphere of gentility and good humor, numerous sailors moved, bearing trays of delicacies from the Japanese trader and generous cocktails. The latter were particularly attractive to the returning boarding party members. Dinner was an unusually sumptuous affair with the glittering opulence pleasing to sight and smell. It consisted of freshly killed venison, broiled chicken, roast pig, and all the accompanying vegetables and fruits. Afterward there was dancing to two ship's orchestras and general entertainment by members of the ship's company.

Through it all the handsome Zuckschwerdt moved as the perfect host with a light word for every lady and a considerate thought for the gentlemen. His rare charm, educated conversation, and elegant manner were in the best form. As the evening wore on Zuckschwerdt escorted his guests around the ship, telling anecdotes, showing pictures painted by crew members, and obviously concerned with his visitors' enjoyment. There was no word about the day's more serious events. As the tired Bartlett took his early leave of the captain, however, Zuckschwerdt did point to a fine collection of Polynesian spears and arrows used in the decorations. Pointedly, if sadly, he remarked, "Those are the only implements of war that we have on board, Bartlett." This tiny allusion was the sole reference and went unnoticed in the general frivolity. Zuckschwerdt stood by the gaily decorated gangway and spoke a personal goodbye to each departing guest, wishing them every good fortune. Even the weather cooperated—the return trip was akin to a fairy tale in itself as the landing barges glided over the moonlit, phosphorescent, soundless water to the land.

Late that night a coded message arrived from Washington, clarifying the earlier one—the United States had broken diplomatic relations with Germany. Governor Smith, who had enjoyed the party along with everyone else, immediately ordered all German personnel on shore back to their ship. There was an equally prompt shift in American-German relationships, making the party a splendid memory marking the terminus of a happy period. Within twenty-four hours Smith isolated the *Cormoran*. The crew was not permitted off the ship, beyond a mail orderly and the few men charged with picking up required provisions on shore. This latter group could not move beyond the landing pier since American work parties now brought the supplies to the dock area and dumped them in the general area. The troops from the garrison occupied all the gun positions in the harbor and trained the various antiquated weapons on the *Cormoran*. There was a constant day and night control of the harbor, with unscheduled patrols prowling about looking for wayward Germans. In the interests of security Smith held up all cable communications to the ship. The near-crisis of February 3, the arrival of the unexpected and suspicious Japanese goods, and the normal laws of human addiction to rumor combined to create a genuine fear of the Germans in the island community. Within a few days the civilians heard many tales of the raider's military prowess and ability to destroy the island and its inhabitants.

The following weeks were filled with general expectancy and

fervent preparations, by both parties, for hostilities. On the American side there was a fundamental concern about taking the ship intact and the ultimate housing of her captured crew. Smith never doubted his ability to overwhelm the *Cormoran*, but he was uncertain about the captured crew. The sole prison available at the moment was the ship herself. At the same time Smith was positive that Zuckschwerdt would either attempt an operation against the cable station as a possible defensive bastion or quickly scuttle the ship. Given the peculiarities of Apra Harbor, the structure of the outer reef shoals, and a general water depth approaching twenty fathoms, the Germans could scuttle their vessel without difficulty. Nonetheless the governor held daily conferences, seeking plans for saving the raider. As his staff completed each plan, he always demanded a new one. Smith did not want any possibility to escape his notice.

Ultimately he presided over a final conference on April 1 which assembled an operational scheme. It provided a meticulously detailed concept. Once the news of war arrived in Guam, Bartlett and Lafrenz would visit the *Cormoran* with a simple demand for unconditional surrender. If Zuckschwerdt agreed to this ultimatum, the ship's ensign would be lowered and replaced by the American national flag. With that signal, waiting vessels, towing sampans, would move alongside the ship and take on the crew. All officers would be taken off by the first boat and transferred to the futuristically named concentration camps. The one, Camp Barnett, would serve the officers; the other, Camp Asan, would house the other ranks.

If the *Cormoran* elected not to accept the governor's requirement, the departure of Bartlett and Lafrenz should serve as the general alert signal for all guns. When the official launch reached a predetermined position, well out of the line of fire, a designated battery in the area would fire the first shot. With this signal all other available weapons should open fire as well. When the *Cormoran* put up the white flag, all firing should cease immediately while Bartlett reboarded the ship for her surrender. The Americans were ready.

By strange coincidence the Germans completed their final preparations on the same day. Zuckschwerdt had realized the new circumstances when the friendly atmosphere changed so abruptly. While his knowledge of international events was now fragmentary, he assumed that war must be imminent. In accordance with his long-standing operational philosophy he assembled his officers in mid-February and went over their precarious situation and the alternative solutions. He dismissed escape as an outright impossibility. The Germans simply did not have sufficient coal or any chance of locating a sufficient supply. By staying in Guam they limited their options to the two anticipated by Smith. They could attack the garrison or scuttle the ship. While the former choice proffered an honorable end he thought it foolish to needlessly sacrifice human lives. Even if they captured the island, which might be possible after a bloody fight, they could not hold it nor would Guam's resources permit a long-term escape. As difficult a problem in Zuckschwerdt's mind was the simple fact that the Americans had the initiative. They would have the first knowledge of any declaration of war and the obvious advantage of surprise. Without a dissenting voice he ordered the *Cormoran* prepared for destruction.

A large demolition charge was already at hand. It had been aboard since the early days at Tsingtao and had been concealed from the Americans throughout the internment period. Bartlett had come close to surprising them on February 3, but he had not observed a false panel covering it in one of the coal bunkers. The ship's engineer, with a few sailors, quickly prepared the charge and placed the electrical igniter in the captain's bedroom. Then Zuckschwerdt demanded additional measures to ensure the ship's destruction. The crew dismantled the bilge pumps, prepared the removal of essential pieces from the ship's power plant, and assured easy access to the valves necessary for scuttling the *Cormoran*. On April 1 Zuckschwerdt made a careful survey of all the preparations and congratulated the participants for their work. Thereafter, each day, he insisted upon abandon-ship drills. These would be initiated by the code word "Cormoran." The Germans were ready.

With both sides prepared, everything was ready for the possible declaration of war. The news reached Guam just after 6:00 A.M. on April 7 in a terse cablegram. Captain Smith had it decoded and telephoned Bartlett in his quarters. In a quiet, measured voice he said, "Please come to the office, Bartlett." The latter, obviously aware of the probable ground for the call, hurriedly dressed and drove to the governor's residence, arriving about 6:50. Lafrenz appeared shortly thereafter. Smith handed them three sheets of paper. His sober quietude revealed their basic contents. The first was an order for them to proceed to the *Cormoran*, since a state of war existed between the United States and Germany. They should demand the surrender of the ship and, if the captain agreed, arrange the specific terms, if not, they should point out that the Germans would be treated as enemies. The second document was a simple note to Zuckschwerdt informing him of the war's outbreak and demanding the surrender of his ship and crew. Smith spelled out this requirement in his final paper, a four-point capitulation program: 1) the ship's personnel to become prisoners of war; 2) promised settlement of the issues involving private property; 3) the transfer of the ship to an American prize crew; 4) the strict conformity with the rules of war. Having provided the essential documents Smith shook hands with his two youthful representatives and wished them luck. They hurried out the door, climbed into a waiting automobile, and drove off to the landing at Piti.

Aboard the *Cormoran* Zuckschwerdt was also awake and suspicious. Several days earlier, in conjunction with the authorities on shore, he had scheduled a temporary change in the ship's anchorage. The shift was to take place that morning at eight o'clock. At 6:30, however, the captain of the *Supply*, W. P. Cronan, who had already received the war announcement from Smith, informed the ship's duty officer that the *Cormoran* should remain in her current position until further notice. Smith understood that he could deal more easily with a ship at her moorings than with a maneuverable vessel under a full head of steam. The duty officer immediately appraised Zuckschwerdt of this change. While a change of mind was not irregular nor unusual the cancellation notice was unusually urgent and intemperate. The captain dressed promptly and was on the bridge before 7:00. He quickly noted the movement of the *Supply* to a position near the harbor's entrance and the shifting of smaller boats throughout the harbor. His fears at least partially confirmed, Zuckschwerdt ordered a prompt alert of all personnel pending developments.

Bartlett and Lafrenz reached Piti shortly after 7:30. Awaiting them was Lt. W. A. Hall, whom Smith had designated as the prize master for the German vessel. He had a crew of eighteen together with a marine guard of fifteen, already assembled and waiting additional instructions. The two emissaries provided none, but did comandeer two signalmen with their flags for speedy communication with the shore in the event Zuckschwerdt gave up without a struggle. The governor's launch was ready, with a white truce flag stretched taut by a stiff breeze and a new ensign especially broken out for the event. With a quick wave of the hand they were off, Hall's group following in a larger, slower barge. As Bartlett's craft headed around a projecting point into the main ship channel it encountered the small boat of the *Cormoran* towing a barge to shore for provisions. It was in charge of Lieutenant Gebhard who had just married an American nurse on Guam. Because of his marriage he had permanent charge of the boat so that he could speak to his wife on the occasion of a shore visit. In passing, the unsuspecting bridegroom saluted smartly and hurried past toward his hopeful, marital encounter. He did not notice that Bartlett neglected any return salute.

As he stood in toward the channel, however, Gebhard encountered Hall's boat some distance away. Hall realized that war had been declared, that the launch had a German officer in command, and that no one knew what would happen aboard the raider during the ensuing minutes. On his own initiative, then, Hall decided to fire across her bow, to heave her to, and to capture the minuscule prize. He ordered marine Cpl. Michael B. Chockie to fire a shot well ahead of the German boat. As Chockie complied with the order, he actually fired the initial American round in the First World War. Gebhard apparently did not hear the shot and paid no attention. Hall then detailed Cpl. J. M. Yelton to fire as well. The two marines began to fire on opposite ends of the German launch, drawing their shots closer each time. Gebhard finally hove to, in obvious surprise over his unexpected reception. The time approximated 7:55. Before Hall could either explain his action or capture Gebhard, events elsewhere intervened.

Bartlett and Lafrenz reached the *Cormoran* at almost the same moment Hall initiated his pursuit of Gebhard. Bartlett climbed aboard alone, while Lafrenz pushed off to a nearby observation point on the starboard quarter. As Bartlett reached the deck he found only a single, very junior officer to receive him. The normal, daily shipboard activities involved with maintenance were not taking place; a clear indication that the Germans knew something was amiss. Everyone anticipated an important event. Requesting permission to speak to the commanding officer, Bartlett was escorted immediately to the captain's quarters. As he moved along the deck, Bartlett noticed the German ensign fluttering in the early morning breeze. This was unusual for the time since normal procedure dictated raising the flag at 0800 hours. Bartlett remembered, then, that if other warships in the area were underway, custom dictated that all ships would raise their flags—regardless of the time. The *Cormoran*, obviously attentive to custom, was merely complying with custom. This same tradition demanded that a flag flying before 0800 would be lowered briefly just before that time and then raised to full staff again.

When the German flag came down at 0759 the curious observers ashore, totally unaware of ship customs concerning flags, assumed that Zuckschwerdt had surrendered the ship to Bartlett. They anticipated the final act of raising the American flag. When the crew hoisted the German ensign back to its proper place the onlookers were confused as to what had happened aboard the *Cormoran*.

The totally unaware Bartlett went on with his business. Entering the cabin, he found Zuckschwerdt and two other officers. He noted that every porthole framed an interested face. Everyone was patently concerned with the momentous event. Bartlett addressed Zuckschwerdt, "I have a letter to present to you, Sir," and handed him Smith's brief note on the commencement of hostilities and the surrender of the ship. The German captain read it without comment and passed it on to the other witnessing officers. When the missive was returned to him Zuckschwerdt asked, "Have you another officer with you to hear my reply?" Bartlett responded, "There is an officer in the barge [*sic*], but it will not be necessary to have him present to hear your reply."

Zuckschwerdt slowly moved around his visitor, softly mumbled a word to a crewman standing at the door, and closed the entry as the sailor disappeared on deck. As the door snapped shut Bartlett heard a great commotion outside. The faces at the port holes vanished and the thud, thud, thud of hurrying footsteps sounded outside the oppressive stillness of the room. Together with the sound of moving men could be heard the mingled shouts and cheers around the constantly repeated word, "Cormoran," "Cormoran." Turning back to Bartlett Zuckschwerdt said quietly, "In reply to this letter I state that this is an unarmed and defenseless ship, incapable of resistance. I am willing to turn over the officers and crew of the *Cormoran* to your charge, but I cannot turn over the ship." Bartlett, seeking to avoid delay or misunderstanding, addressed the fundamental issue at hand, "I am not authorized, Sir, to discuss terms other than as stated in the letter just presented to you. I am here to accept the immediate and unconditional surrender of the officers, the crew and the vessel under your command." Zuckschwerdt refused any alteration in his stated position, "In reply I repeat that I am willing to turn over to your charge the officers and crew of the *Cormoran*, but I cannot and will not surrender the ship."

Bartlett responded with the only solution open to him, "Then I have to inform you that when your answer is received you will be treated as an enemy and your vessel as an enemy vessel." Zuckschwerdt simply inquired, "Is that final?" "It is final." "You have my answer." The American saluted, turned, and left the cabin. No one said anything in farewell or friendship. As Bartlett moved toward the main deck he heard the excited crew yelling, over and over, "Cormoran," "Cormoran," and observed all hands running aft along both sides of the deck, cheering as they ran. Pushing his way to the gangway, Bartlett saluted the uncertain junior officer standing there and signaled the expectant Lafrenz to pick him up. As the launch sped alongside Bartlett jumped aboard while the boat was still in motion and ordered Lafrenz to make speed back toward the island. The latter had already observed the ship's colors being lowered as he moved forward and was surprised at Bartlett's unusually peremptory tone. He asked, "I thought that you were going to stay on board if she surrendered?" To his amazement Bartlett replied, "She did not surrender." As they pulled away from the ship they could also observe the flag, once more at proper station and the intense activity of the crew running along the decks. They were busily throwing things into the sea—boxes, life preservers, planks, trunks; a veritable shower of material.

As soon as the American left, Zuckschwerdt ordered all secret material destroyed, restated the destructive password, and gathered his complete crew on the quarterdeck. He notified them in a few succinct words about Smith's ultimatum for unconditional surrender, a demand which he had refused even to consider much less accept. As his final order Zuckschwerdt ordered the crew, following dismissal, to quietly leave the ship from the stern. He concluded with three cheers for the kaiser. Immediately the crew began jumping over the side. An onshore observer likened their departure to a shimmering white sheet extending from the ship's deck to the water. The non-swimmers, sick, and the Chinese, who had no love of the water, climbed into the sole available lifeboat. Zuckschwerdt also ordered the sole prisoner held in the brig released until such time that matters could be settled in proper order. (He received a pardon.) Lt. Dieter Reger, who had charge of the destruction, quickly turned the electrical ignition in the captain's bedroom. The resulting shock rocked the boat, but no more.

Bartlett's launch, some 100 to 150 meters away, felt the muffled explosive wave just as the occupants heard a deep, dull, heavy detonation and observed a red flash slowly pulsating upward to the height of the masts. Pieces of debris shot high into the air, curled over, fell. A heavy smoke trail drifted lazily upward into the sky. The ship settled slowly by the stern, and then listed some ninety degrees to starboard before she went down with a rush. Just before disappearing she was capsized on an visible level keel. All that remained was a suspended column of water hanging like a theatrical curtain, a foaming, seething area of surface disturbance with a broken piece of errant flotsam shooting upward like a flying fish and falling back with an awkward splash. In between were three small boats and heads, dozens of heads, bobbing here and there, dark specks in the shocked waves. While high overhead circled a covey of pigeons released from the ship. Confused by the sound and destruction, they hovered, circled, dipped, and coasted, frustrated symbols of the peace destroyed with their home. A further incongruous note in this curious scene was that many crew members had remembered to bring along a bottle of spirits to combat the water's ravaging cold. Clinging to wooden boxes, hatch covers, chairs, and life jackets, they drained flasks of all hues and shapes. Then a musician, Heinz Farkens, true to his calling, raised an oboe, almost a submarine periscope, in sound. Everyone joined his dissonant voice in a ragged, but clear, "Deutschland uber Alles." The *Cormoran*'s death was a proud one—worthy of her traditions.

In another tradition of the sea, the last man off the ship had been the captain. He stood on the guard rail by the flying ensign and paused briefly to observe his ship. It was precisely four years, almost to the day, since he had assumed command of the *Cormoran* in Sydney, Australia. As he jumped into the water he could see the rudder and the silent propeller poised for the final descent. Once in the water he had no opportunity to consider the vagaries of fate which had brought his command to this bizarre end. There were dozens of men to be fished from the water and placed in safety.

Fortunately for all concerned the Americans moved with enviable dispatch in rescuing the swimming men. Hall, who had in the interim captured Gebhard's boat, promptly freed his prisoner with the words, "Go ahead and save your crew." Gebhard hurried back toward his sinking ship, throwing overboard all excess materials in a frantic effort to lighten his boat. He was back at the spot where the *Cormoran* had gone down within ten minutes. En route he encountered Bartlett's launch moving at top speed toward Piti. Gebhard called out, "You turn around and come too, Mr. Bartlett." The latter fully intended to comply with this injunction, but first, he shouted orders that Hall should land all unnecessary men forthwith and mount a rescue mission in the bay.

Showing considerable initiative in the surprise and confusion Bartlett tied one of the sampans to his launch and sped back with it. Once near the center of the swimming men, he cut the sampan loose and let it float through the general area. The water remained in a grotesquely turbulent state. Overall, however, reigned Zuckschwerdt. He had managed to swim to the *Cormoran*'s motor boat and ordered it here and there throughout the area, shouting directions, moving floatable materials toward laboring swimmers, picking up the weakest men. Clearly he was in charge of events. Everyone yielded to his authority, and even the Americans answered his commands with the disciplinary promptness expected in all navies. When the *Supply* moved into the area as well, her commander, Lieutenant Commander Cronan, even saluted before offering his assistance. Shortly after nine o'clock the searching boats moved ashore. The *Supply* kept up the search until 9:55 when Cronan finally gave up as well.

Zuckschwerdt had already reached land, but not without a final adventure. As his small boat reached the dock and discharged a few weak sailors, the captain ordered the engine destroyed. The engineer, Arthur Deubert, seized a large sledge hammer and completely demolished the machinery with a few hard blows. A marine sentry, observing this destructive activity, sighted his rifle on the engineer's large shoulders. As he fired, a nearby marine officer struck the rifle's muzzle, deflecting the man's aim, and the shot went harmlessly into the sky. It was an instinctive action, befitting a day where kindness replaced hatred between the new foes. Even in conflict some men retained a measure of decency toward their fellow unfortunate human beings. The violence of the *Cormoran*'s warship was over, but the United States was unquestionably at war. This brief encounter provided the first violence, the first Germans killed in action with the United States, the first prisoners of war, and the first shots between the United States and the German Empire.

In the explosion, the subsequent immersion in the water, and the uncertainty of rescue seven men lost their lives. The searching Americans recovered six bodies. In each case Smith insisted upon a proper funeral with full military honors. Zuckschwerdt conducted each ceremony and consistently endeavored to bring back the splendid words of the proud parson in Majuro Bay on August 29, 1914. As well he praised the men of the U.S.S. *Supply* and the crew members who had performed so many acts of heroism in helping other comrades in the water. A simple cement monument, erected by the Germans, was placed over the graves with the inscription, "They gave their lives for the honor of the flag."

For the survivors the future was relatively simple. From their water-isolated freedom they journeyed to a land-bound prison. As soon as they were ashore the Americans ferried them to the two prison areas in the few elderly Model T Fords on the island. This automobile chain often broke down and, more often than not, the German mechanics had to repair the vehicles taking them to prison. Since the camps were not entirely finished, the prisoners fur-

nished most of the labor for their completion. Within the barbed
wire and watchtowers they laid out areas for physical training,
gardening, walking, and simple pleasure. Within a fortnight they
planted trees and flowers making their prison into a confined
pleasure spa rather than an evil fortress. The men had learned the
methods of close living. The Americans treated their captive
friends with meticulous care. They made certain that authorized
pay allowances were continued properly, that individual belong-
ings were returned expeditiously, and that personal needs for
clothing were furnished from local naval stores. The married
personnel received local accommodations outside the collective
compound.

After three weeks of such tolerable confinement, however, an
American transport, the *Thomas*, arrived at the island and removed the crew to the mainland. After a long, arduous sea voyage
via Manila, Nagasaki, and the Aleutian Islands the ship reached
San Francisco. The local authorities, despite their distant removal
from the submarine war, feared possible popular recriminations
against the prisoners. They hurried the men on to a comandeered
ferryboat to Oakland where they placed the prisoners of war on a
train to Fort Douglas, Utah. Subsequently the authorities transferred the enlisted men to a camp near Fort McPherson, Georgia,
where they remained for the war's duration. They reached Rotter-
dam, on October 7, 1919, aboard the S.S. *Pocahontas*, and,
through the aid of the Dutch authorities, crossed the border at
Wesel. They were home.

Eventually Zuckschwerdt returned to Germany where he went
on to a distinguished naval career. All the other crew members
went back to Germany excepting three of those with American
wives who elected to remain in the United States. Of the others
the South Sea Islanders remained for awhile as local curiosities.
These muscular visitors provided curious sights to all as they
strolled about in their long skirts, oddments of German equipment, and curious language usages. They enjoyed employment
for several months on land clearing projects. As well, however,
they enjoyed observing the local scene. When one viewed the first
motorcycle he had ever seen he suggested, "He come, he stink, he
go." At a huge, island-wide community affair in July 1918 they
performed various exhibitions of spear throwing and native danc-

ing. They were the star attractions! In January 1919, through the courtesy of the United States Navy, they returned to New Guinea.

The Chinese received their choice of destinations. Rather than seek return to Tsingtao they elected to remain in Guam and to open a laundry. They were a most welcome addition to a community where cleaning was still conducted by the ancient and difficult beating of the clothes on stream rocks. The Chinese rapidly became prosperous through their industry and lived out their lives as small testimonials to the progress possible in war. The lessons of the *Cormoran* were not lost.

Bibliographical Note   **Index**

Bibliographical Note

Surprisingly, few authors have attempted the serious study of the *Cormoran*'s history. The most valuable materials come from the various archives. On the German side there are a number of brief narrative accounts prepared for official use. The best are those of the captain, Adalbert Zuckschwerdt, Lt. Hans Muller, and Korvettenkäpitan Oswald Collmann from the *Planet*. In the German archives are also a few brief studies from various crew members and a number of related documents. Of these materials the most interesting is a critical study by an unknown person after the war. It may well have been the later chief of the German navy, Erich Raeder, who wrote *Der Kreuzerkrieg, 1914–1918* as vol. 3, pt. 1 of the official history, *Der Krieg zur See, 1914–1918* (Oldenburg, 1931).

The American documents are contained in three basic files. Unquestionably the most valuable is Record Group 45, "Naval Records Collection of the Office of Naval Records and Library— Subject File, JT, 1911–1927, relating to the German Cruiser, *Cormoran*." It contains all the fundamental records of the raider's existence on Guam. Also useful are Record Group 80, "General Records of the Department of the Navy General Correspondence No. 9351–19395: 28–80, relating to the German Cruiser, *Cormoran*," and Record Group 24, "Records of the Bureau of Naval Personnel and the [incomplete] Log of the U.S.S. *Supply*." There is limited information in the annual reports filed by the governor of Guam.

Published accounts offer only sketchy details of the *Cormoran*. The best is Owen Bartlett's account of the sinking, "Destruction of the S.M.S. *Cormoran*," *United States Naval Institute Proceedings* (1931), pp. 1044–51. Although his brief account of the ship's early history is not well done, Bartlett drew his story of her demise from his own official reports. Julian S. Corbett's *Naval Operations*, vol. 1, *To the Battle of the Falklands, December, 1914* (London, 1920) contains a few limited remarks for the official British account while Arthur W. Jose presents a fragmentary, argumentative survey in the *Official History of Australia in the War of 1914–18*, vol. 9, *The Royal Australian Navy* (Sydney, 1941). Other limited details may be found in the German *Der Krieg zur See, 1914–1918*, vol. 7, pt. 1, *Die Kampfe in den Kolonien* (Berlin, 1934).

A few limited odds and ends are available in Otto Brauer, *Die Kreuzerfahrten des "Prinz Eitel Friedrich"* (Berlin 1918), Franz J. Hohenzollern, *My Experiences in S.M.S. "Emden"* (London, 1928), and Paul Carano and Pedro C. Sanchez's *A Complete History of Guam* (Rutland, Vt., 1965). Herbert Ward's *Flight of the "Cormoran"* (New York, 1970) contains an account of the ship's adventures but concentrates on the author's salvage activities with the ship—efforts which eventually resulted in his death diving on the hulk.

Many general studies of the naval war mention the *Cormoran* but none of them include a satisfactory account of her activities. A felicitously written study in Keith Middlemas, *Command the Far Seas: A Naval Campaign of the First World War* (London, 1961). Edwin Hoyt has written various popular books which help create the atmosphere of the times. One can consult *Kreuzerkrieg* (Cleveland, 1968) and *The Last Cruise of the "Emden"* (New York, 1966), as examples of his work. Many writers have pursued the *Emden* with limited success. A. A. Hoehling's journalistic *Lonely Command: The Story of the "Emden"* (New York, 1957) provides an example of the genre.

The same may be said of the major naval battles in the Pacific. Many writers have pursued the subject but no one has completed the task. Geoffrey Bennett's *Coronel and the Falklands* (London, 1970) provides a graphic description which may be a correct version. A happy opinion is that of Hans Pochhammer, *Before Jutland: Admiral von Spee's Last Voyage. Coronel and the Battle of the Falklands* (London, 1931).

A splendid dissertation is that of Albert Ganz, *The Role of the Imperial German Navy in Colonial Affairs* (Ann Arbor, Mich., 1972). The author lacks a specific direction but he provides much useful information on German thinking and activity in the Pacific. Charles Burdick *The Japanese Siege of Tsingtau* (Hamden, Conn., 1976) attempts a description of the city during the First World War. John Schreker's *Imperialism and Chinese Nationalism: Germany in Shantung* (Cambridge, Mass., 1971) gives a fine account of Germany's interest in and governance of that area.

Strangely, Osgood Hardy and Glenn S. Dumke's *A History of the Pacific Area in Modern Times* (Boston, 1949), while out-of-date in many ways, remains superior to the more recent histories of the area.

The volume, *Germany in the Pacific and Far East, 1870–1914* (St. Lucia, Queensland, Australia, 1977) edited by John A. Moses and Paul M. Kennedy contains an assortment of papers concerning its subject. It does merit every consideration because of contributions from the editors. Kennedy discusses archival resources in minute detail while Moses appends a select bibliography of impressive scope.

Index